> Behold also the ships, which though they be so great, and are driven of fierce winds, yet are they turned about with a very *Small Helm*

Small Helm Press interprets direction in contemporary life

Pearl Evans

DANCING WITH THE TIMES
What's a young adult to believe!

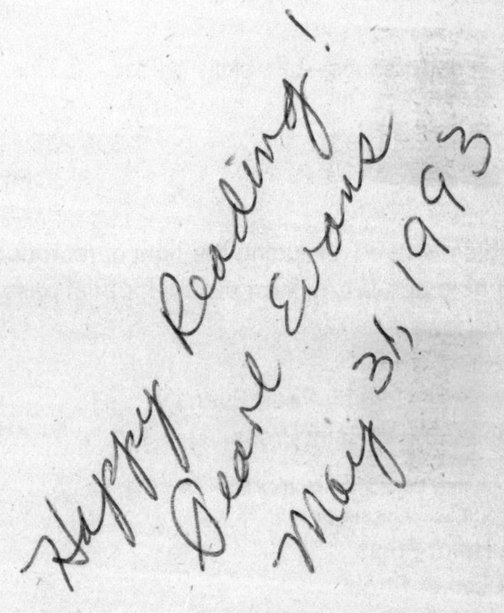

Small Helm Press
Petaluma, California

Publisher's Cataloging in Publication
(Prepared by Quality Books Inc.)

Evans, Pearl.
      Dancing with the times : what's a young adult to
believe! / Pearl Evans.
      p. cm.
      Includes bibliographical references and index.
      SUMMARY: Helps young adults deal with contemporary
influences that can destroy life or give it meaning.
      ISBN 0-938453-05-X

      1. Young adults—Life skills guides. I. Title.

HQ796.E92 1993   305.235
                                              QB193-613

Copyright © 1993 by Pearl Evans
Design by Small Helm Press

This book may be ordered by mail from the publisher.
Please add $2.00 for shipping:
Small Helm Press
622-A Baker Street
Petaluma, California 94952-2525

Manufactured in the United States of America

Library of Congress Catalog Card Number: 93-92656
1 0 9 8 7 6 5 4 3 2 1

FOR

Nealy, Jesse, Kelly, Kerry, Kristin,
Justin, Andrew, Melissa, Kurt,
Rachel, Jordan, Geoffrey, and Sue

ACKNOWLEDGMENTS

To Cynthia Horkey
To Loren Chin, photographer
To friends who critiqued the manuscript

ON THE COVER

Young adults from rear and left to right:

1. Mike Chou
2. Matthea Ma, Mpho Chuenyane,
   Stefan Cleveland, Heidi Grimm
3. Rick Esponda, Matthew McCarthy

CONTENTS

A. BECOME AWARE OF INFLUENCES OF THE TIMES

Not knowing whom to trust is like dancing through a minefield

B. CHOOSE YOUR INFLUENCES

Sam's sophomore year
FEELING

Following your feelings is like dancing on the freeway

Sam's junior year
THINKING

Thinking like the times is like dancing with a bulldozer

Chapter 1

Where Are You Headed?
Not knowing whom to trust is like dancing through a minefield

Sam Ming smiles as he reads from his private journal about his junior high days—for as a senior, he sees that he has worked out his eighth grade problems. And although he continues to meet new challenges, he has learned a lot about how to deal with them. In the pages ahead, we will follow sharp Sam and his inquiring ethnic friends through their high school days to discuss the issues of their lives and yours. Here's what Sam reads:

Dear Sands of Time,

I've got lots of questions. Sometimes what I hear everywhere makes sense. But if that makes sense, then what Mom says doesn't make sense. But I don't want to talk to her about it unless I have to. On the other hand, it might feel good to let her know I can think for myself. I mean, I learned at school that if you believe something, you should act on it. That's the part that bothers me. When I'm just now putting out feelers about all these things, I don't think I'm ready to act on them. Even if it sounds exciting to take risks like we talk about at school, I know I'd hurt Mom if I turned against what she believes.

So here I am caught in the middle, not even sure what I think. But one thing I know. I don't want the guys to put me down. Look what happened to Jim. In class in our small group's discussion, when he talked about marriage and family like he was sure what he believed, Bob laughed. But worse yet, a lot of kids said he shouldn't talk about right and wrong because that meant he was putting down some kids and their parents. One of them has a mother who has a live-in boyfriend. And several have divorced parents. And no one even listened when Jim said he didn't mean it that way.

The worse part was that the others made Jim out to be like someone who can't think for himself. They said he couldn't back up what he said and so that meant he was just copying what his folks believe. He was supposed to prove he was thinking for himself, but he couldn't. I know Jim felt rejected, but he kept his cool. I've got to give him that much credit. Actually, I sort of admired him for what he said, but I didn't let anyone know, not even Jim, even if he is my friend. I don't feel too good about not backing him up, but then again, what if he's wrong?

Although Mrs. Jones always lets our group talk without interfering, she did tell Bob not to make fun of anyone. But I could tell the damage was already done. And Mrs. Jones did say that different people have different ideas. I was glad to hear her say that because I was afraid she might send Jim out of the group because I know the rules. If anyone is judgmental, he has to leave the group.

Since my Dad died, I wonder especially because when Mom and I argue, it's just me against her. And who's to say which of us is right? The trouble is Mom doesn't buy the "conflict resolution" I hear about in class. She doesn't see us as equals. She thinks somehow that she is my "authority," and she says it like she means it. She usually listens to my side, but when we can't agree, I have to do it her way. That's why I'm always asking her, "Do I have to?" because sometimes even when she wants me to go one way, she lets me choose the other.

Mom means well, I think, but still I'm not sure I want to go her way even when she says I have to. I mean it's always been hard to go along with what she wants; look how strict she is. And what makes it even harder is that everyone says I should go ahead and do what I want to do—that I'm a different generation. But I don't know about that... I'm not sure of anything.

And at school, I have an even harder time because I don't know what to say in our discussion group. I'm not sure I want to spill my guts there even if the teacher says not to clam up. I haven't got anyone to talk to because I know how Mom feels and I know how Mrs. Jones and the school counselor feel. They let all us kids know we can talk to them about personal problems any time we want to. And they give us names of agencies and phone numbers and all that stuff, too. But I'm not sure whether I want to join their side or stick with my mom for now. I know Mrs. Jones would say I don't have to choose between them, that they just want to give me a chance to talk things out. They say that, but I know their ideas clash with my mom's. Besides, I do care about my mom even if I do get mad.

That's why I'm writing you, Sands. At school, I have to write in my journal, but I don't want to let Mrs. Jones know that I'm not going along with her necessarily either. I mean, who wants to ask for trouble? So here I am. And that's all for now.

Sam and you become confused because adults are confused. It used to be different. In another generation everyone in the community taught you right from wrong the same as your parents at home. Even movies, magazines, books, and popular songs gave the same general message. Can you imagine a kid on the way to school singing to himself a popular tune like *Dear Hearts and Gentle People* about hometown adults? Quite a different message from *Cop Killer!*

Of course, not everything then was good nor is everything now bad. But in those days, at least teens knew when they were doing wrong and many of them would later get back on track. Now without people to guide you in a clear way, you can destroy yourself before you have a chance to find your way.

The culture of the past is gone and you as a young person get little input to bridge your way over to it. The fact is that most of what you hear about the fifties and earlier are just nostalgia stories that can only make you feel a sweet sadness about days that are no more. And so your own roots may seem more foreign to you than the culture of Russia or Africa because those cultures are still in progress right now and you study about them at school. I'm here to fill in the blank spots of your knowledge about your own present and past and to show you that from one generation to the next some values never change. And I dare to say they anchor you to what is beautiful, lasting, good, and lifesaving.

So I want to be your babushka. Did you know that babushkas, Russian grandmothers, probably had more to do with the fall of the Berlin Wall and the Soviet system than conservatives or liberals in America or Gorbachev in the Soviet Union or even the collapse of the Soviet economy? All those may have played a part, but freedom would have been impossible had not the babushkas worked behind the scenes for seventy years, undoing the work of the communists. The leaders themselves admitted these beloved women were a problem. All day the youth learned Soviet doctrine, but then later babushkas worked with them to straighten out their thinking—sometimes far into the night. They showed youngsters which influences were harmful and how to resist them. In a no-nonsense way, they taught them how to tell right from wrong. And in an atheist land, they kept alive the spark of what is sacred.

You're surrounded by harmful influences, too, even if you can't see them and even if you're not aware of them. So you need a guide, but who? *Not knowing whom to trust is like dancing your way through a minefield of hidden explosives*, which are waiting for you to step on the spot that will set off a blast. Of course if you know where the danger spots lie, they lose their power. For then, stepping around them becomes as safe and easy as stepping around someone's prized petunias. You don't have to be afraid, just careful; that's all. When you walk through a minefield, whom you trust to show you the way makes a difference. Once you learn this, you will choose your influences consciously and carefully.

To get through early adulthood, you dance with the times but on your terms, not with blind, unquestioning agreement.

Chapter 2

THE POWER OF SUGGESTION
Following your feelings is like dancing on the freeway

Sam's Sophomore Year—Chapters 2 - 7—FEELING

In feeling-centered times, sophomores Sam and Joe and fifth grader Marie learn about the power of suggestion and altered states of consciousness.

"I would have gotten here sooner, Joe, but I daydreamed my way past the turn," Sam says as he kicks down the stand on his bicycle.

"Space-Man Sam. That's my Chinese friend!"

"American friend."

"You look Chinese to me, Sam."

"The only time I feel Chinese is when I look in the mirror. My ancestors have been here so long I think they must have come over on the Mayflower."

"Yeah, sure."

"How about you? Do you feel American?"

"Why shouldn't I?" Joe asks.

"You look Hispanic to me."

"That's just how I look, Sam. I'm like you. I speak American, I think American..."

"Say, Joe, are we going to break out that new Space-Man electronic game, tonight?"

"No, my mother has other plans for us. We're going to a seminar tonight."

"You're kidding!"

"No, I'm serious. You remember how my mom got involved in that human potential group? She wants

us to hear this speaker talk about the possible harm involved with altered states of consciousness so we won't get messed up like she did."

Later at the meeting, the speaker, Steven Smith, describes daydreaming as one kind of altered state. Joe pokes Sam. "That's why you missed your turn. You were in an altered state of consciousness."

Smith lectures:

You usually pay attention to the outside world, but sometimes you change your focus. You turn away from what's going on around you to what's happening inside of you. That change of focus is a changed state of consciousness, or an altered state of consciousness. You lose your awareness of the outside world.

"That was me all right," whispers Sam to Joe. "That's me in math class."

You wonder why you should be interested in knowing about a changed state of consciousness? You should care because in an altered state of consciousness others have a lot more influence over you than they otherwise would have.

In daydreaming, you enter an altered state on your own. But suppose someone else changes your state of consciousness. Then that person can plant suggestions that influence you because your mind is passive, not alert.

This person can also control and influence an audience. He talks to them in a low voice and keeps talking along in this way with a well con-

trolled voice in a carefully paced way in a monotone. And he keeps talking, and doesn't change
the pace or the tone, and everyone listens. That's
how he gets control of the audience.

*Seminar speaker Smith—by his pacing, tone, and
style of speaking—demonstrates how such a person
controls an audience. Sam notices what's happening
because he saw a speaker on television put an audience into a light trance. So he looks around. Sure
enough the audience is subdued, including Joe.*

"Joe," Sam whispers as he elbows him.
"Huh?"
*"You were out of it. Don't let the speaker do this
to you."*
Later Smith returns to the soft talk routine:

You are paying attention to what I am saying.
Everything is fine and going along well. And you
are going along with what I am saying...

*He goes on and on. Everyone is quiet, and Sam has
to jolt Joe again. They laugh quietly together while
they look around at the dazed audience.*

So you see, you fell into a light trance even
though I told you earlier what I am doing!
If you want to know when someone is manip-
ulating you and the audience, you need to study
both the speaker and yourself. Watch for a
speaker who talks quietly in a monotone, sing-
song voice in an evenly paced, soft, soothing way.
Or look for the opposite—a situation where the

speaker has to talk above a lot of noise so that you have to strain to listen. And check yourself, too. See whether you are very relaxed or very "hyper." If you are either, you are more likely to be swept into an altered state.

You are at your best in an audience when you keep yourself in a frame of quiet alertness, attentive but distanced from what's happening, but still that's no guarantee you won't be affected. The only way to break away from going into a light trance is to turn and talk to the person next to you or to get up and walk out of the room.

"I guess you did the right thing by punching me and making me talk," Joe says to Sam after they beat the crowd out the door.

"Yeah. If I hadn't known something about this before, I wouldn't have been so amused, and we would have been taken in like everyone else."

Later Joe's mother, Mrs. García, puts cups of steaming hot chocolate on the table for the boys and fifth-grader Marie and then comments, "That was a form of hypnosis you experienced tonight."

"Not us," says Joe. "We resisted."

"Well, don't get too smug. The art of suggestibility has been fine tuned these days. Someone can influence you more than you realize just by the way that person speaks or gestures."

Sam sweeps his hands toward Joe and fixes his eyes on him. "You are going under, under, under..." Joe drops his head forward as though he has been zapped.

"I know all this sounds far out. All I'm saying is

to be alert to someone who seeks to gain your trust," says Mrs. García. "For example, to gain that trust, a person may try to become more like you, and reflect the way you talk and act. Suppose Sam uses a lot of touching kind of words. He might say, 'Things feel real HEAVY in my life, and I can't HANDLE it. Maybe you can GRASP what the problem is.' Then the other person would answer with more touching words and say, 'You feel WEIGHED DOWN, don't you?' Or Marie might use a lot of seeing words."

"I SEE what you're talking about," Marie says.

"Let's FOCUS on this together," Sam says. "

"Let's try it with some hearing words now," Mrs. García coaches them.

"I HEAR what you're saying," says Joe.

"Let me CHIME in," says Sam. "What you're saying RINGS A BELL. You're saying that someone can influence us by acting and talking in sync with us."

"Influence," says Mrs. García, "begins with someone gaining your trust and ends with your acting upon that person's suggestion."

"The power of suggestion," Sam adds.

"Someone can get you to believe something untrue," says Joe, "and make you bark like a dog."

"I'm not talking about staged hypnotism, Joe. That power is pretty obvious. I'm talking about everyday persuasion. That's what you have to watch out for, influence that can get you to do something: join a group, change your values, change behavior."

"Ask my mom," says Sam. "A salesman talked her into buying encyclopedias." Everyone laughs.

"Let me tell you a way that's not so ordinary, a way that can set you up for an altered state of consciousness," Mrs. García continues. "Someone has you imagine a scene and leads you through it by describing what's happening."

"Uh-oh," says Marie.

"What's the matter?" asks Mrs. García.

"I think maybe that's what happened at school last week."

"What happened?" her mother asks.

"We have this exercise we do everyday. It's called Stages. It's really sort of fun. I never thought anything about it until just now."

"Does it make you feel relaxed, maybe like you're floating?"

"Yeah, that's it."

"Tell me more."

"Well, most of the exercises are fun, but one day we did a sad one. We were supposed to think about some sad things."

"Like what?"

"Okay. I'll take you through it," Marie says. "All of you do what I say. Uncross your legs and put your feet flat on the floor, put your hands in your lap with your palms up. Sit up straight but relax. And close your eyes." Marie's audience complies. "Do you see that cloud? It's coming down toward you."

Marie begins to talk in a slow, dreamy voice with her eyes closed: "Okay, now get on it. Can you feel how soft it is?" Sam and Joe, with eyes open, pat the cloud as if to fluff it up and smile at each other.

"Okay let the cloud take you as high as you want. Then peek over the side at all the things going on down there on the earth. Can you see anything that makes people sad?"

Joe peers over the edge of his imaginary cloud and says, "I see school Monday."

"You can't talk, Joe. That ruins it." Joe puts on a serious face. "Do you see that little girl crying? Her dog got run over by a car. And she just moved to this house, and she has no friends. She had to move because her mom and dad just got a divorce. The cloud keeps moving and you keep looking down. Now you're going over the ocean. You see a lot of bodies on the shore. They're big; they must be seals that died because of all the pollution in the water. And you see someone in a boat going up to a whale. Then you see a flash; it's a spear hitting right between the eyes of the whale. You keep floating along on the cloud.

"There's a factory down there and something is pouring out of it. They are chemicals, and you can see that ducks are dying. You keep floating. Now you're over a town and you see litter on the streets. You're still floating on that cloud, over the forests now, and up ahead you see smoke.

"All these things make you feel sad, and you wonder what you can do about them. Maybe you should make a poster that will help people not do all these bad things, and then the world will be a better place. Your cloud is drifting down, down, down, ever so slowly. You are coming back to the kitchen now. You get off the cloud. And now we are all back, sitting around the table, drinking hot chocolate."

Sam shakes his head several times as though he's coming out of a trance.

"You made that up, didn't you, Marie!" says Joe.

"No, I didn't. The only part I made up was about the ducks. And our class didn't come back to a kitchen and hot chocolate."

"Cold chocolate now," Sam corrects her.

"Marie remembers what happened," says Mrs. García. "If she had forgotten the experience, she might not have known why she felt like making a poster when she got back."

She pauses. "Here's what I want you to notice, folks." Everyone looks up at Mrs. García. "This was supposed to be a relaxation exercise about personal feelings, but it's more than that. Can you see that an exercise like this could be used to affect how you feel about some issue?"

"Yeah. I see what you mean," Sam says. "The power of suggestion influences you without you realizing it."

"When you're in an altered state," says Joe, "you receive suggestions much more than you would otherwise. Isn't that what the speaker said tonight?"

"So what should I do, Mom?" asks Marie.

"You don't have to put yourself under that kind of influence."

"Will you write me a note before you forget?"

Follow your feelings? Not necessarily.

Nor do you have to be fearful about influences.

Instead do like Sam, Joe, and Marie:

1) Become informed.
2) *Monitor* your reactions—that is, stand back from an experience to examine it.
3) Find those who can support you in resisting this kind of influence and be a support to them.

Glossary words are usually italicized.

Chapter 3

ACTIVITIES AND AWARENESS
Following your feelings is like dancing on the freeway

Sam and Joe talk about feeling-centered activities: meditation, visualizing, magic thinking, role playing, guided imagery, and spirit guides. Sam is gathering material for a class project.

"Pssst... Joe, over here," whispers Sam as he motions Joe to come sit at his table in the library. "Look what I found." Sam shows Joe a book. "This gives a different slant about altered states of consciousness from what you usually hear. It's more like Steven Smith."

"Let me see what you found." Sam slides the book over to him. "Hey, my mom talks about some of these: meditation, relaxation techniques, visualizing, magic thinking, role playing, guided imagery."

"The author says these are not just fun and games, that some are good but some aren't."

"You mean he says they're dangerous?" asks Joe.

"I don't know. I haven't read that far. I just read the first part about euphemisms."

"What are euphemisms?"

"Those are words you invent to make something sound better than it is. They're word substitutes with a new spin, you might say. Here. Read for yourself."

Joe looks at euphemisms for meditation: "Stress management, centering, concentrating, higher order thinking, awareness and relaxation techniques."

"Do these sound like Eastern meditation to you?"

Sam asks.

"No," answers Joe, "they sound like things people want. Who doesn't want to learn to relax, to concentrate better, and to think in a higher order?"

"That's what euphemisms do," says Sam. "They make something unacceptable sound acceptable... Now let's read this part about Transcendental Meditation." They read the following silently:

One form of meditation of the times is Transcendental Meditation, or TM. Barry Robertson, a former TM instructor says that to empty your mind in TM, you repeat a word called a mantra over and over. "At first," Robertson says, "you don't even know that you're experiencing this transcendental consciousness. You can't remember it; you can't grasp it. But as you do more and more meditating, you become aware that you are aware of nothing... You are able to experience that nothingness, that emptiness. You can peer down into it." You become detached from life like you're watching a movie. You "dissolve," Robertson says.

Reaching this state made life seem strange to him, however. He began to sense things about people and to see pastel colored auras around them. He was also disturbed about practices within the group and felt trapped. Finally, when in desperation Robertson prayed to God, the strangeness stopped, and two weeks later he found the will to walk away a free man.

"Sam, that guy was lucky to get loose from that."

"You know it."

Later after the two read the section on visualizing and magic thinking, Sam says, "I visualize. I practice my diving that way."

"Run me through it, Sam."

"I see myself on the diving board. I wait, breathe in as I rise up on my toes, breathe out as I come down again, take the right number of steps to the end of the board—all this has to be with the right timing—come down hard at the right place, and shoot myself high into the air, touch my toes before I start down, straighten out, and enter the water without a ripple."

"You mean you can do a jackknife?"

"Not yet, but I can visualize it."

"Get out of here, Sam," Joe says as he slaps Sam on the shoulder. "Do you do magic thinking, too?"

"No, and I wouldn't even dabble in it, Joe."

"Me neither, but I can see why someone might fall for it if they didn't know it was something from the occult. My mom says people get into it because they want to make things happen their way. That's why they chant and cast spells."

"Yeah, they think they can create their own reality," says Sam.

The book's next section is about role playing. Sam and Joe laugh about actors who have to give up roles because the actors identify too strongly with the characters to be able to continue playing them.

"Listen to this, Joe: 'The actor that played Maxwell Smart on television found himself acting out in real life some of the idiot behaviors of his series character. He finally had to give up the part.'"

"That's a riot, Sam. Can't you just see him somewhere taking off his shoe and talking into the hidden microphone in the heel?"

"It's funny on television. It might be embarrassing in real life," says Sam.

"Then there's Jim Bachus. He had to quit his impersonation of the voice of Mr. McGoo... These professional guys have problems, but I don't freak out," says Joe, "—like when I play the role of your customer so you can practice a sales pitch on me."

"You're harder to sell to than real people."

Sam and Joe learn that feeling-centered activities range from good to bad. Some activities, like meditation, put you into an altered state. On the other hand, visualizing to practice a skill like diving or selling can be helpful. Then again, if someone guides you through a visualization, that can be harmful.

In role playing, the danger comes when you begin to think and act as if you are that character. If you play fantasy games for long periods of time, you may find it difficult to separate fantasy from real life. And when your fantasy mixes with the occult, you may even be influenced toward murder and suicide. That is rare, but there is another more common danger. Records show that role playing sometimes triggers emotional reactions that can interfere with your life.

After reading the next section of the book about guided imagery activity, which often includes spirit guides, Sam releases a soft "whooo..."

"You must be reading that information taken from a 1991 Santa Rosa, California newspaper," says

Joe. "That's where it says this man Pierre Creager claimed he looked to a spirit guide for guidance. And he hammered a woman to death with a hammer."

"Yeah, that's spooky stuff."

"What do you expect from a spirit guide?" asks Joe.

"You know what scares me off from spirit guides," says Sam, "is that people who practice guided imagery warn others how dangerous it is. Right here. Look what Marilee Zdenek wrote in the front of her guided imagery book." Sam points to this passage:

PRECAUTION: Never use any of the exercises in this book when your attention is required by small children or others who are dependent upon your alertness. These exercises should never be used in a location that could be dangerous. A person who is emotionally disturbed should not use these, or any other techniques for dealing with unconscious material, except with the help of a professional therapist.

"And do you notice," says Joe. "she even puts the warning in capitals and italics so you won't miss it."

"But the fantasy sounds so harmless: the beach scene and the travel on the train, the rhythm of the engine, the fog, the colors. You know what that reminds me of?" asks Sam.

"The visualization Marie told us about."

"So you thought of that, too."

"The difference," says Joe, "is that Marie's visualization didn't have a spirit guide in it. Zdenek has you meet some kind of living creature; that's the spirit guide. Listen:"

You let something wonderful appear before you, something alive. Now it speaks to you. You can get to know this dream character in any way that you please... And there's something important that you can learn that will have great meaning to you in the future.

"My mom told me," says Joe, "these activities might have a spirit guide appear as a friend, a child, an old man, a Martian, or a rabbit or some other animal. It can be any creature that you talk with in your dream state."

"Joe, there's something else that shows an altered state can be more than ordinary daydreaming. In guided imagery, Zdenek tells you how to return after your trip. She says it takes a while to come out of it, to change from the dream state to the thinking state. The way I see it, if you have to be waked up when you're not asleep, that means you've crossed over into something more serious."

"And don't forget the danger we learned about at the seminar," says Joe. "If you get into an altered state, you're open to what someone else feeds into your thought life."

Sam closes the book, leans back, breathes deeply, and says, "I know there are dangers, but you can't deny this: When you read Zdenek's guided imagery story, it still seems harmless."

"Sure does. It's deceiving."

There's one point Sam and Joe didn't make. Even aside from questions about spirit guides, if you think your own imagination can be your guide in life, you hang your future from a very thin thread. You need a better source for guidance than that.

And don't think you and even adults in your life can escape having to deal with these influences—in business, government, education, the military. For example, in 1992 a civilian employed by the military told me about an activity called "The Presence," part of a required seminar. She didn't understand the activity's purpose, but she knew enough to know it was strange: Participants sat and stared into each other's eyes. The technique she told about seems to resemble a Scientology cult activity, which a former Scientologist described this way: "They sat me down across from this other guy. They told us it wasn't staring, but it was simply staring at each other—two hours that first night... At first it was very uncomfortable. We sat with our knees touching and we weren't allowed to blink. We were told, 'You don't think, you don't move, you don't twitch, you don't giggle. Just be there with the other person.'"

You don't need to understand something fully to see that it's bizarre and serves no good purpose. That's enough for you not to participate. Your parents may have you excused. Or if something is upsetting or somehow doesn't feel right and you are caught without warning, you can be the one to remove yourself from an activity, film, or play. The daughter of a friend was so bold.

Follow your feelings? At times, but don't empty your mind.

Chapter 4

GROUP POWER
Following your feelings is like dancing on the freeway

Feeling-centered activities usually take place in groups, which in themselves influence powerfully.

Sam comes to Joe's house to play the electronic game the two didn't play on his earlier visit. But first they prepare their "Group Power" social studies assignment.

"Why isn't Marie around tonight?" Sam asks Joe.

"She's having a serious talk with Mom."

"In trouble, huh?"

"No, she feels bad about what happened in school today. The teacher asked her class to pick out someone that doesn't fit in with their group. They chose Denise."

"Is that the little girl everyone makes fun of?"

"That's the one."

"They couldn't help her?"

"I think this time it was a case of the medicine killing the patient," says Joe. "Denise had to stand in front of the class while everyone wrote on a slip of paper what it is that they don't like about her."

"So how does that affect the way Marie feels?"

"The students didn't just hand Denise the papers. They read their papers out loud. By the time they finished, Denise sat there crying."

"That is strong medicine, I'd say."

"And that's not the end of the story. When Denise was walking home, her classmates beat her up and

said they would never like her."

"Marie didn't beat her up, did she?"

"No, she feels bad for Denise. That's why she wants to talk to Mom."

"Joe, you can use that incident in our class discussion about group power tomorrow."

"But it's so personal, I don't know..."

"Just leave out the names and places."

"Somebody might figure it out though, and that might hurt Denise some more."

"Yeah, you're right... I've got something I can tell about. It's about some people that live in another town. In this group home, a kid I'll call Harry knows how to get things stirred up. He leads the other boys in raids and riots."

"How does he do that?"

"Well, one time after a counselor got on his case about something, he went into action this way. While the counselor was talking to all of them, he put on this big act like he was bored." Sam demonstrates as he talks. "He lay back in his chair, looked up at the ceiling, lolligagged, and then dropped his head forward like this, like he was asleep."

"And the kids cracked up," says Joe, laughing.

"Of course. Then all of a sudden Harry jumped out of his chair and gave a whoop: 'Follow me guys.'" Sam keeps acting out the story as he talks. "He leaped across the room without looking back, and every one of those kids landed his feet in Harry's footprints."

"It would be pretty hard to get things back together after that, Sam."

"By that time, no one could stop them. The guys followed Harry up on the garage roof."

"Oh, no."

"And from there they started loosening bricks and throwing them into the yard."

"What are you going to say about that incident in the discussion about group power, Sam?"

"That it's as contagious as measles."

"What is it that's contagious?"

"Good question. What's contagious?... I know. Rebellion is contagious."

"You're right, Sam. Just hearing you tell the story makes me see those kids take off. And if I was younger like them, I'd probably be right behind them."

"Who are you kidding? Not you, Joe! Maybe Lucas."

"Okay. So, I'd feel like it anyway, especially if you were the kid leading the riot."

"Now that's a different story. If you just sat there like a statue, it would take the steam out of the whole thing. Maybe nobody else would follow me either. In fact, that's probably what would happen if I tried something like that... Hey, what kind of friend are you anyway, raining on my parade?"

"Don't get mad at me for something that never happened. I started off this fantasy by saying I'd probably be right in there with the rest of you."

"Joe, that's another good point for the discussion tomorrow. If you didn't go along with us, it would be like you were condemning what we were doing."

"Yeah, I don't think those boys thought about what they were doing. Sam, they just felt that red blood flowing through their veins, and they took off."

"So that's another point about group power," says Sam. "In a group you don't usually think about what's right and what's wrong. You just do it."

A group has that kind of power, sometimes even with adults in charge; look at Denise. And does it surprise you that in group discussions, those who get attention are the rebels, risk-takers, and jokers? Paul McGhee, Texas Tech University, who has studied humor for fifteen years, confirms this. He says children who joke, laugh, and clown are often leaders—that they use humor to pull people's strings. But can you count on that kind of person to lead you right?

Sam gets to the point: "Let's get this schoolwork out of the way so we can get to the game. Tell me about your book. Then I'll tell you about mine, and we'll be all set to give reports tomorrow. And let's don't interrupt each other, or we'll never get to the game."
Joe stands up and gives this report:

My group power report is about *Among the Thugs* by Bill Buford. To write his book Buford spent weekends hanging out with these young British hoodlums who were soccer fans. Those Europeans take their soccer seriously. So if their team loses a game, everyone comes apart. They riot, they rob, and sometimes they kill. And this doesn't happen just once. It keeps happening all the time.

I said these men were hoodlums. Actually, they were ordinary guys that had jobs. They were guys that lived in nice neighborhoods. But put them together at a soccer game, and look out!

Buford said that these guys had to work themselves up to a peak moment before they exploded on the scene. They'd start by chanting something like 'Liverpool, Liverpool'—that's a place in England. And they'd do that until something clicked. And that was it! Maybe it would be something like someone shattering a window pane—anything that would get the adrenalin going, and off they'd go.

If you met one of them, you'd like him, but put him with the others and something demonic seemed to take over. That's group power. And Buford found out he wasn't immune either. He got carried along with what was happening. This is what he wrote: "The crowd is in all of us. It is, like an appetite, something in which dark satisfactions can be found." And a reviewer of the book said the fact that the men were so ordinary makes the whole thing that much more scary.

"Your turn, Sam."
"I'm going to refer to my written out report, Joe. I'll work on it some more at home."
"Just get on with it, Sam."

My book is *Ordinary Men* by Christopher Browning. This book is a good example of how the power of a group can influence people to do things they would not otherwise do—terrible things. This was a real horror story. Nazi Germany was a totalitarian country. That means the government controlled everything in everyone's whole life. And your morality was measured by how loyal you were to your group, the Nazis.

Here are the facts: During World War II, 500

ordinary men murdered 38,000 Jewish people and sent 45,000 to their death in the gas chambers, a total of 83,000 lives snuffed out. This was a police battalion occupying Poland. They weren't young, and they weren't street people, and they weren't criminals before. They were family men, too old to enlist in combat troops. They had been workers, sales people, and clerks.

These men had been taught to hate Jewish people, but they had no training for murder. And yet they did it, even though the officer in charge said they could ask to be excused. Twelve men, in fact, did ask to be excused; and others later asked to be excused. But even these didn't say they wouldn't murder because it's wrong. Instead they said they were too weak. *They didn't want to seem to be criticizing their comrades.*

The amazing point Browning makes is that afterwards the men seemed to have no realization that what they did was wrong. And according to Browning, what kept them from facing reality was group solidarity. He says they didn't murder because some leader pressured them to or because they were afraid of punishment. He says they did it out of loyalty to their group and to get ahead in their careers in that group. He ends by saying, if these men could become mass murderers, what group of men cannot? He warns you about the power of the group to lead you in the wrong direction. THE END.

Sam and Joe race to the computer. Joe wins.

Although the Nazi slaughter was part of what is called the Holocaust—the murder of six million Jewish people—still there's an important lesson for ordinary you. It's this: You shouldn't make group loyalty the measure of your morals!

In group activities, be alert. You may be tempted to follow unwise advice from adult instructors, but you're the one who will suffer. Notice those leaders who teach risk-taking in sex and drug classes and who accept whatever decision you make about drug use and teen sex... who encourage you to act on your feelings, to express the dark side of yourself, to break with your past and to consider yourself your own best authority... who belittle moral judgment and overemphasize yielding to group consensus. It's up to you to seek other influence and to swim against the tide of the times.

Membership in a group can become more important to you than lifelong beliefs and your own idea of who you are. And the stronger the tie, the greater the influence. That's why your choice of friends is so important. But a group doesn't have to be harmful to shape your life; it can be any tightly knit group, and it can be an influence for good. Author-Englishman W. Ross Ashby says that the brain arranges itself according to experience. Perhaps something like this happens, he says, when a lot of boys end up being so much alike after attending the same British school.

What's important is for you to realize that as a human being, you *are* influenced. It makes sense therefore to choose carefully those influences you place yourself under and those to which you pay attention.

Follow your feelings? The price for togetherness may be too high.

Chapter 5

DEATH AND SEX
Following your feelings is like dancing on the freeway

Feeling-centered times challenge you to face the reality of sex and death and to resist powerful influences.

Sam and Joe discuss sex, desensitizing, and moral danger.

FIRST, FACE REALITY!

"Joe, you mean we're taking highway 101?"

"Why not? It's not everyday I get my license."

"I know... but the freeway!"

"I want to practice passing. But now that you mention it," says Joe, "I do feel queasy here in the middle lane with all those cars zipping by."

"Yeah, set me at ease, will you? Oh well, I'll get even when I start driving."

"You'd really have something to worry about if I hadn't learned in drivers' training you don't look at the car you're passing. You look at the road ahead."

"What happens if you look at the car?" asks Sam.

"You feel like you're turning toward it and can't seem to help yourself."

"Wow! I'm glad you got that straightened out... Hey, Joe what did you think about family life class?"

"That visiting speaker didn't seem to mind embarrassing Sonja and Tina, did he?" says Joe.

"No, he seemed to go out of his way to call attention to them. Why do you think he did that?"

"My dad says that what he did was desensitize us."

"What did he mean?" asks Sam.

"He says that to protect young people, especially females, public opinion puts up barriers. Then if desensitizing tears down those barriers, there's trouble."

"So there's nothing to protect against things like sexual harassment? ...and rape?" asks Sam.

"Yeah, that's right. And pregnancy and disease, too. My dad says you have to face reality, and he says the reality is if you expect kids to be sexually active, that's what they'll do."

"It's a funny thing, isn't it?" says Sam. "From the way that guest speaker Jay talked yesterday, you would have thought everyone's having sex."

"That's what I thought, but it turned out from Mrs. Johnson's anonymous survey that only one person in the class has had sex. And only five people said they plan to before they marry."

"After class," says Sam, "I heard Cal tell Mrs. Johnson he was relieved because he had thought he was weird for not being sexually active..." Sam pauses. "Desensitize... Oh, now I remember. I came across that word in English when we read about Mark Twain. He talked about how he was desensitized."

"In what way?"

"Well here. I have my textbook with me. Maybe it'll help us understand what your dad means. Mark Twain was a Mississippi riverboat pilot, you know," Sam explains while he looks for the passage. "So here's what he said about the river he loved: 'Now when I mastered the language of this water and had come to know every trifling feature that bordered the great river as familiarly as I knew the letters of the alphabet, I had made a valuable gain. But I had lost something, too. I had lost something which could never be returned to me while I lived. All the grace, the beauty, the poetry had gone out of the majestic river!'"

"Hey, that does connect with what we're talking about, doesn't it? Dad says you lose something when you have sex outside of marriage. He says sex is supposed to be something special, just for marriage, not something ordinary or degrading."

"Hmm. Your dad said that? I didn't know men talked that way."

"My dad does." The conversation lapses while Joe concentrates on traffic. "There's something else my dad said, Sam. He said if you knew your partner had AIDS, would you trust a condom or would you say no?"

"What are the odds for an infected person infecting you?" asks Sam.

"With an infected person, the odds are too high, Sam—even with a condom every time."

"Jay didn't tell us that."

"Or you could put it another way," says Joe. "Are you sure you want to trust your life to a balloon?"

"That's a good one, Joe. Remember in junior high when someone passed out those sample condoms and everyone was making water balloons out of them?"

Joe pulls over to let a semi pass. The car rocks. "How could I forget? I sat through class soaked."

"Joe, let me ask you a hard question... Why don't more adults help us face reality?"

"You know what I think? I think parents and teachers are convinced that kids are going to have sex no matter what anyone tells them."

"It's hard to raise parents and teach teachers these days, isn't it, Joe?"

Sam and Joe talk about moral danger, which to them is like *dancing on the freeway.* You, on the other hand, may have become sexually active before you understood about morality. Don't become discouraged and think that you might as well continue on that path now that you have started. You can choose *secondary virginity,* which means that although you've had sex, you make a decision to stop now and to abstain until you marry.

And if you've engaged in homosexual acts and haven't been able to break free, you can seek help if you choose carefully; but be aware that most current therapy helps you adjust to homosexuality rather than to support you in changing that behavior. Reparative Therapy is one method that supports your desire to change. Others have entered this therapy and now have their own families.

In either case—heterosexual or homosexual—you start over. And if you fail, you start over again—and again and again if necessary—until you find those influences that drag you down. If you can, find individual or group support, but in any case, don't give up. Of course, it's easier to abstain if you do so from the beginning.

To escape moral danger, you need a higher moral authority. Otherwise, you have only shortsighted consequences and feelings to guide you. And that's not enough, says Ted Koppel of television's Nightline. In a speech to university graduates, he gave this reason for not doing wrong: "not because it isn't cool or smart or because you might end up in jail or dying in an AIDS ward, but no because it's wrong!" Moral living simply stated is to live right because it is right.

SECOND, WILL YOUR CENTER HOLD?
Will Sam and Joe live up to their high ideals? Will you? Here's what you have to face from the influence of the times: negative influences about sex and death. No longer topics for the family circle, sex and death now share the public spotlight. And although they gain attention, they lose their significance for they become no more than animal functions.

As suicide, abortion on demand, and *euthanasia,* or mercy killing, become more frequent and ordinary, the trend seems to be to create a good image for death. One woman, opposes the death penalty because she doesn't think death should be thought of as a penalty. And for a young woman who took death education, death became so attractive that she almost committed suicide, she says. And for others, to help them accept death, a 1991 *Harper's* ad offers a wooden Life Coffin to enjoy everyday as a bookcase or as wine storage shelves.

To resist powerful influences toward death, you need to know at least two things. First, know that following your feelings can be dangerous. Of those who try suicide, most are just depressed. And of these, ninety percent never try again simply because they learn that moods are temporary. They learn to wait out down times. Second, you need to value human life. Taking your own life, or even threatening to, is wrong. It's as wrong as taking someone else's life—or threatening to—for you have no right to take anyone's life. Knowing this removes suicide as an option—even if the temptation may come to your mind.

And to resist powerful influences toward sex, you

need to develop loyalty to your future family. If you begin now to be faithful to your future spouse, you'll be faithful throughout your marriage for you will know what commitment is all about. And to stay with that commitment, you need to know that sex control is possible. For no one engages in unlimited sex; under certain circumstances, people abstain. Not too many years ago, teens in large numbers abstained from sex unless they married. Look at the statistics about fifteen year old girls.

> Now - 26 percent engage in premarital sex
> 1970 - 5 percent engaged in premarital sex
> 1960 - a lower percentage
> 1940 - fewer still

Hormones have not changed; attitudes have.

And so as you develop attitudes about family and sex, life and death, you build your character now right where you are. And if you do *your* part in your present imperfect family—whether a single parent home or not—you will more likely succeed in your future family.

Chapter 6

FAMILY TIES
Following your feelings is like dancing on the freeway

Feeling-centered times weaken family authority.

In their own way, Joe and Marie discuss a feeling-centered activity—a conflict resolution technique that challenges family authority.

"Get out of my room, fifth grade pesky-pest," Joe says as he hurls a crumpled up paper at Marie.

"You used a you-message, Joe," Marie sings out to her big brother as she picks up the paper ball and throws it back.

"That wasn't a you-message. I didn't say 'you.'"

"You said, 'Get out of my room' and that's the same as 'You get out of my room.' You're not supposed to tell me what to do. You're supposed to tell me how you FEEL about what I do."

"Okay. Try this then." Joe rephrases his you-statement into an I-message: "When you barge into my room that way, I FEEL LIKE throwing you out on your ear. How's that?"

"That's not a good I-message and you know it, Joe."

"So who's to say I have to go by your playground rules anyhow?"

At school Marie has learned that I-messages improve communication and you-messages often stop communication. She doesn't give up. "Here's what you need to say. 'Marie, you're a good sister...'"

"That's a you-message."

"Let me finish. I haven't gotten to the I-message yet. Besides it's all right to have a good you-message. It's just the bad ones you can't use. Let's start over. 'Marie, you're a good sister, but when you come in here without knocking, I feel like I have no privacy.' See, that's telling me how you feel without calling me names."

Joe looks dumbfounded. "So if you understood all the time how I feel, then why did you butt in?"

"The door was open so I walked through it."

Learning to refocus you-messages into I-messages can be a good discovery. It was for me in the sixties. Yet although the technique helps me communicate, I reject its author's worldview, which says that parent and child have equal status—and that the only power parents should have is to persuade by expressing their feelings. To act responsibly, those in authority have to have the final word with the right to express themselves in whatever way the situation calls for.

The end result of this worldview is to deny parents and teachers authority. And for any worldview to deny them authority is also to strip away their accountability. This confuses and harms both you and society. *For if you as a young person become convinced that authority has no right to exist, you put at risk your present life and your future family.*

How important is authority in your life anyway? Maybe the best measure is to see the pain caused by the breakup of family authority through divorce. The following is a condensed version of a letter that a daughter made up to help her father understand her family's feelings after divorce, which she compares to the pain and injury of a car crash:

> Dear Dad,
> I want you to know how I feel about what's happened.
> Mom was driving. Then this car came out of nowhere and hit us head on. And dad! I saw you with another woman in the other car, and you just kept going!
> I'm in the hospital writing to you because I have lots of time to think about everything.
> All of us are hurting real bad. What about you—do you wonder about us? Do you hurt, too? Are you going to come see me?
> And do you want to? I want you to.
> We all miss you. Do you think we'll get well?
> Love,
Daughter

This is not just individual pain. This is family pain and goes beyond the moment. A child of divorce is more likely to have emotional problems or learning disabilities; more likely to commit suicide or crime. And the problem doesn't stop there: Divorce passes on broken lives to future generations.

And what the sweep of this destruction from a high divorce rate proves is how necessary a healthy family unit is for the good of everyone. And so now positive signs hover on the horizon. Psychologists less often suggest divorce to couples as a solution because some of them now see the problems divorce creates. Also, couples have learned from experience that living together is not the same as commitment to marriage.

Marriage is different because it is not a human invention; it's built into who we humans are. And yet people of the times invent new ways to look at the family. They say family is any group of people living together or any group of people who care about each other. And because such a group is called a family, then people of the times demand that you accept unmarried living arrangements as moral and call you bigoted—or narrow-minded and prejudiced—if you don't say such behavior is moral.

At the same time other negative forces work in your life. Adult leaders who influence your life become gatekeepers of information, power holders in your life able to receive information from you and to withhold that information from your parents if they so choose. And according to psychologist Jay Haley, this interference can upset family authority and create unhealthy conflict. He points to nature to show that all creatures organize by rank. And by this he supports the natural authority of parents in the family. He goes a step further to say that respect for authority is as basic to American life as the right to dissent, or disagree.

Society, however, increasingly questions the ability and authority of parents to raise their children. Peter Jennings reflected this attitude. On an ABC radio and television special about AIDS and students, he asked a highschooler, "Is it easy for you to talk to your parents about sex?" When the young man answered no, Jennings moved on to interview others. Finally, as if saving the best for last, Jennings returned to the young man to find out more about his problem parents. But it turned out there was no problem. "I believe in *abstinence*," the youth explained. "I've talked with my parents before. And since I have information, I don't need to be talking a lot to them about sex." So, though not by design, a rare teen-abstinence message hit the airwaves. Further probing by Jennings yielded only more good words for the parents. "If I feel the need to talk to my parents, I know I can go to them," the young guest said.

To be like this young man, unashamed of the standards of your parents, appreciative of them, and bold in what you say, is to nail down your future—like Al, the son of a friend. He knows how to stand against the intimidation of the times. His Catholic school teacher asked him: "Are you going to believe everything your parents tell you?" "Yes," Al answered point blank. "I'm going to believe everything my parents say and everything the Catholic church teaches me. I'll listen to you, but I want you to listen to me, too."

Knowing the teacher's overbearing ways and knowing quiet Al's shy reluctance to speak up in most classes, his schoolmates recognized his fearlessness in this incident. Although Al was not seeking popularity, he became a school hero. And although he was not trying to outdo the teacher, his peers declared him winner. The school buzzed with, "Hey, did you hear about Al? He set back Mr. J. Doe a peg or two."

To be on the offense, not on the defense, heads off trouble. And there are also practical things you need to know about dating and your future.

Chapter 7

YOUR FUTURE FAMILY AND YOUR PRESENT LIFE
Following your feelings is like dancing on the freeway

Sam and Cecelia listen to a school assembly speaker:

The speaker reads a letter from a high school girl, who writes about her friends: "'I sat and cried with each of them a few weeks after their first time and prayed with each of them that they weren't pregnant.' The writer's three friends planned to marry their boyfriends some day, but none of them did. They broke up with them a short time later. The letter writer was spared that heartache because she had no serious boyfriend at the time. From this she learned that sex is no promise of marriage. She concluded her letter: 'Now I know without a doubt or regret that I will experience the joys and wonders of sex only when I am married.'"

Afterwards Cecelia says to Sam, "I'm glad they had this speaker today; it makes me feel better about my own ideas. No one else tells kids that sex for them is wrong. My biology teacher gives us the idea that remaining a virgin isn't popular and certainly not desirable."

"Yeah, same in family life class."

"The pressure to be sexually active," says Cecelia, "comes more from adults than from students. You know what really helps me see things straight is to see what happens to my classmates."

"Yeah," says Sam, "seeing someone else mess up

is what made me decide which way to go. I saw my cousin and his girlfriend have to change all their future plans because she's pregnant. Unfortunately, my cousin learned his lesson too late."

PRACTICAL HINTS TO PROTECT YOURSELF AND YOUR FUTURE FAMILY
Sam and Cecelia find out they can learn from the mistakes of others, as can you. Another way you can protect your future is to avoid what leads into a destructive lifestyle. Habitual sexual activity and drug addiction don't develop full blown overnight. First you choose friends with questionable standards. Then you begin in small ways with wine coolers, beer, smoking, marijuana, softcore pornography, small time gambling, or other gateways to bigger trouble—all of which lead to influences that weaken your determination not to have sex outside of marriage.

And although all these lead to family trouble, pornography is especially dangerous to you as a youth because it affects your sexual life. Lesbian pornography draws young females into lesbianism and other porn targets young males from twelve to seventeen because they are the most responsive customers. Pornography twists your ideas so that sex becomes a way to express hate, not love, and some porn fuels the despising of Jewish people, Christians, and others. Also, research shows that a young person has a greater desire to imitate behavior in pornography than do adults. And most disturbing, the younger a person exposed to this material, the more he desires to act it out. That's why molesters use pornography of both sexes to condition young persons to perform sex acts.

To avoid these early steps to danger, you can choose

to abstain from alcohol, drugs, pornography, and so forth. But what about uninvited influences that you don't care to have? For that you need to find ways to handle damage control. For example, this strategy works for my purposes: As a writer who reads widely, when I come across offensive words and passages in books I own, I ink out what is offensive. In this way I express my resistance to the influence and can enjoy the books later when I refer back to them.

Highschooler Eve knows how to handle damage control. While in line to give the coach her written excuse for sitting out physical education class, she heard the crude remark the coach made to the girl in front of her. Since Eve's excuse was the same as that of the embarrassed girl, she knew she had to do something to stop the coach from humiliating her. So she did the only thing she could think of. She looked him straight in the eye and said in slow and even tones, not loud but deliberate, "Don't say a word!" And he didn't. He didn't dare! And since it turned out a short time later that the man was fired from teaching because of sexual misconduct with a minor, Eve did well to draw a clear line for limits. It's up to you to let others know when they overstep the line of respect for you.

And this is important. To go beyond just damage control, you need to avoid putting yourself in dangerous situations. The obvious precaution is to avoid isolated locations in single dating and to avoid parties where you know there will be drugs and alcohol. In college you can join a growing minority of students who choose to live in campus housing that requires a pledge to abstain from alcohol. Or in some dormitories, you can ask for nondrinking roommates.

To prevent problems listen to Kathleen Honeycutt, guest family life lecturer. She says if you are female, you can become aware of signals you send that can be misinterpreted as invitations for sex—how you dress, how you talk, physical messages, such as putting your hand on your boyfriend's knee, snuggling up close. *You* may mean to be friendly, but that may not be the message your date gets. You want to be sure you give a clear message. There are ways to let your date know you care without misleading him.

And if you are male, here is a question typical of what teens ask Honeycutt: *"How can a guy handle the situation when a girl makes moves on him on a date?"* (Or in reverse, when a guy makes moves.) She explains that you should prepare ahead of time to avoid trouble. She compares this situation to driving a car. Before you drive a car, you make sure it's trustworthy. If it's not, you find other transportation. When you go out with a girl or boy, make sure the one you choose is trustworthy. Know what your date's values are and make sure that one knows yours.

"Where do you draw a line on a date?" is another question couples ask. Honeycutt lists the stages in a relationship. (Compare where you draw the line with the upside-down discussion at end of chapter.)

1- Holding hands
2- Kissing
3- Necking (from the neck up)
4- Petting (beyond)
5- IT
6- End of relationship.

You need to keep in mind what dating is all about. Besides having fun, the idea is to get acquainted with members of the opposite sex, to find out how to relate to each other, to learn what qualities you value in others, and to learn more about yourself. Aside from the moral question, to allow sex to become part of the dating scene throws everything out of perspective. Such involvement keeps you from seeing your dating friend in a clear light and confuses you about what commitment means.

KEEPING A CLEAR FOCUS ON YOUR FUTURE FAMILY

To steer a straight path to your future family, you need to keep a clear focus on what you want. Many young people, in fear of failure, give up hope for a happy home. That was true for Lynda Barry until she came under the influence of a neighbor, about which she wrote in a *Newsweek* article, "Guardian Neighbor."

The kids on Lynda's street had a ritual. They would steal other neighbors' flowers to hide behind their backs, then present them to their favorite neighbor, Mrs. Yvonne Taylor. She'd give each one a tight hug and express her surprise and delight. The influence of such spontaneous joy was almost unknown in the troubled homes where these kids lived.

Mrs. Taylor influenced Lynda in another joyful way the day Lynda asked to go to church with her. There something happened. They went to a Baptist church in an old store with hanging light bulbs and beat-up chairs. She noticed the people talked sort of loud and laughed. It was the music, however, that hit Lynda so hard. "Forever after," she said as a youngster, "to hear any music, even Farmer in the Dell, makes me remember the music that 'got me,' and I can't keep from crying."

But that's not *the* influence that hit Lynda hardest. It happened the day she stole over to see Mrs. Taylor at dawn. "I stood on her porch knocking and knocking and knocking, weighing how much of a bother I was becoming against how badly I needed to see her."

She told Mrs. Taylor that her mother said she could have breakfast with their family. Mrs. Taylor laughed. What was different about this visit is that the whole family was together, and they were in their bathrobes, kidding around. Mrs. Taylor put her hand on Mr. Taylor's shoulder as she poured coffee, and he leaned his face down to kiss that hand.

"And that was all I needed to see. I only needed to see it once to be able to believe for the rest of my life that happiness between two people can exist," Lynda wrote. That's all you need, a glimpse and a conviction. For if you see clearly a family in your future, you will reorder your whole life in the direction of that vision. You will change the way you otherwise might live for then you set your sexual life apart for its special place in marriage.

To see something clearly is to gain wheels, wind, and sails to go in the right direction. A vivid picture of family propels you toward influences that carry you toward your goal and away from influences that would drag you down.

Follow your feelings? No, you're the leader.

Chapter 8

YOUR CULTURE

Thinking like the times is like dancing with a bulldozer

Sam's Junior Year—Chapters 8 -13—THINKING

Now a high school junior, Sam is alert to radical influences. His interest began in junior high when he learned about influences harmful to his culture.

Here's what happened two years ago in ninth grade:

After an exam in his last class, Sam leans back in his desk, glad to relax with a silent film about the environment. He smiles to himself as he watches baby ducks gliding along in the water behind their mother and little birds in their nests waiting with their mouths wide open. He can almost breathe in that fresh air and feel the sunshine on his back.

He's unprepared for what happens next. A huge, yellow bulldozer bursts on the scene, rips apart shrubs and grass, gobbles up soil, shoots dust into the air. A camera zooms in. "AMERICAN," says lettering on the side of the bulldozer. From it jump two men. One pours out gasoline; the other lights a match. Flames explode. Animals scatter.

Ducklings, now on the bank of the creek, burn alive while Sam watches, stunned, helpless. Trees crash, spilling out nests right into the path of the monster, which plows under and runs over the little live birds and the charred remains of the ducklings.

At the end of the scene, a sentence flashes on the screen: "Man cannot foresee or forestall. He will end by destroying the earth."

When Sam gets home, his mother knows something is wrong. "What happened?" she asks as he throws down his books. He tells her about the film.

"Shall I ask Bill Updire to come over? He might help you."

"Good idea! I like talking to Bill."

"We haven't known him very long, but you two seemed to hit it off at that summer youth study group. He's a professor, but he seems to be on the same wave length with you high school kids."

When Bill joins Sam at the kitchen table, he asks for all the details. Afterwards he looks out into space while he leans his chair back on two legs. Then he looks at Sam and asks, "Why do you think the camera zoomed in on the lettering on the bulldozer, Sam?"

"To show the company or maybe where it's made, I guess."

"Could there be any other reason?" Bill asks as he brings the chair to rest and leans forward toward Sam.

"Well, now that you mention it. I guess we do hear a lot about how much damage Americans do to the environment. So I guess that wasn't meant to be just the name of a company. It was supposed to be just another jab at us Americans. You warned our study group that we might run into hate-America stuff."

"Anything else you might notice from what you've already told me about the film?"

Sam takes some time to think. "Well, yeah. That bit about man destroying the earth. My mom says some people try to make human beings to be like just another species of animals, only not as nice as the other species. I guess that's what that statement flashed at the end makes you think when it says that man will destroy the earth. It's like humankind is public enemy number one."

"I think you're right."

Bill pauses. "The film upset you, didn't it?"

"Yeah." Sam ducks his head. "How would you feel if you had to watch a whole ecological system go up in smoke?"

"Not good. Not good. Interest in the environment is a good thing, of course. We ought to think of the future. But there's something that bothers me..." Bill explains to Sam how political activists use scare tactics to gain political power: the nuclear threat, in the past a threatened ice age, now overpopulation.

"But that's not my main point now, Sam. I want to show you the bigger picture. The film you saw makes me think of a good illustration for something else I want to get across to you. Something basic and really important... You learned in earth science that an ecological system has a delicate balance. It needs the right kind and number of animals, the right kind of vegetation, the right kind of streams."

"And fresh air and clean water. No pollution."

"The same kind of delicate balance applies to people, Sam. Just like the natural ecology is fragile, the cultural ecology of people is fragile, too. I'm talking about the fragile social culture of people... Do you know what I mean by culture?"

"Sure, in class we talk a lot about culture. You mean everything about the life of a group of people—their customs, their language, their way of looking at life, their government. What I want to know though is how can a culture be fragile? Are you telling me it's breakable?"

"Yes, it's breakable like the ecology of the environment is breakable. Mess around with one part of the network of relationships too much and you ruin the whole thing."

"Tell me how that works."

"There was a time earlier in the century when cities decided they had to do something about their run-down neighborhoods. They didn't like the way everything grew up helter skelter. The best thing city planners could think of was to plow under bad housing and old fashioned buildings and start again from scratch."

"Sounds like a good plan to me, Bill."

"Sounds good all right. That's why they went ahead and did it."

"Hey, I think I see the connection. I can see the wrecking ball tearing down all those buildings and that terrorist bulldozer sweeping through the neighborhood just like that bulldozer in the film swept away everything in front of it... And now you're going to tell me the plan didn't work. Right?"

"Right."

"What happened?"

"Sam, now listen up. This is important. You know that country scene that you saw destroyed? Those men could destroy that ecology, but they can't build it up again. They didn't set it up in the first place. It's something like that with people ecology—social systems, neighborhoods, culture, traditions."

"But people do build up neighborhoods and traditions."

"True. People build culture and social systems, too.

And they even plan for them. But no one group and no individual and no government can create what makes up a society. Everyone is part of the chain of events and the networking. No one creates or invents the total picture of what we call a culture."

"So what happened when they bulldozed those neighborhoods?"

"They could destroy them—they could and they did—but they couldn't rebuild them. It didn't come out right. The high-rises replaced houses and apartments and put a lot of people together who then had to drive a long way to their work. The streets got crowded; the automobiles polluted. Community spirit disappeared. Nobody knew their neighbors; the mom-pop stores were gone. People didn't sit outside together on the steps on hot days."

"But what can we do about run-down neighborhoods? We can't let them just go to seed, can we?"

"No, we got smart. We realized that we have to make changes as we go along without upsetting the whole system. Now cities preserve neighborhoods and restore them that way or make some improvements here and there."

"So what am I supposed to learn from this?"

"This point: that radical change—extreme change, that is—can do a lot of damage. Our society needs liberals on the left and it needs conservatives on the right. It doesn't need radicals or extremists that want to bulldoze our society."

"Down with radicals." Sam points thumbs down.

"Well, let me revise my statement. As a society, we do need radicals. Not only should we allow them freedom, we should be able to see that they play a

necessary part in the big picture."

"We need them," says Sam, "like the environment needs snakes and bugs, huh?"

Bill laughs and says," Not exactly. Radicals are human beings, and in a free society we do need them. They shake us up and get us moving and make us figure out what we really believe about things. But since they can destroy and can't rebuild, what we don't need to do is to follow their radical advice."

"Spell it out for me, Bill. Where do they go wrong?"

"Their big mistake is to build on a false foundation, and that's why in the end they fail."

Two years after this incident, Sam as a high school junior is alert to influences that play upon his emotions for *ideological* purposes. Although he hasn't lost his sensitivity to environmental destruction, he now refuses to be manipulated. Therefore, he'll check out for himself what he hears. And he'll watch for the big, yellow bulldozer of *totality thinking*, which totally destroys existing culture to build a radical new one.

Influences destructive to American culture work in many ways. So instead of having to learn the details of all of them, you can concentrate on learning what is good about your culture. Bank administrators apply this principle in teaching tellers to recognize counterfeit money. Instead of teaching them to recognize all possible counterfeits, they teach them the feel of genuine money so that they can recognize anything different. In the same way, if you learn what makes America great and good, then you can recognize a distorted viewpoint of your culture, the American one.

Think like the times? Think again.

Chapter 9

CULTS, TOTALITY THINKING, AND INFORMATION
Thinking like the times is like dancing with a bulldozer

By learning about cults, Sam learns more about the destructiveness of totality thinking.

"Mrs. García, how did you get mixed up with a group that had such strange ideas?" Sam asks.

"I'll tell you this, Sam. This group didn't come to me with a big sign telling me they were a cult."

Sam is shopping at the grocery store with Joe and his mother. They're going to have a wiener roast.

"What is your definition of a cult anyway, Mom?"

"You can define cults different ways. When I talk about cults, I mean destructive ones. So I don't define them by their teachings but by their total control of the whole life of a group of people."

"Would that be like the totality thinking that Bill talks about?" Sam asks.

"Yes. Totality thinking begins with the illusion that a group knows what is good for everyone else and therefore should control them."

"Did you read about those people in that cult in Waco that fought off the federal agents and killed four of them?" Sam asks. "I'd never fall for anything like that."

"Marshmallows?" Mrs. García asks.

"Of course," Joe answers. "You can't have a wiener roast without roasted marshmallows."

"Sam," Mrs. García answers him, "you could fall

for a cult just like anyone else. Smart people, dumb people, rich people, poor people are all easy targets at certain times in their lives, especially when you're young."

"But you wouldn't join a cult like the one shooting at people, would you?" asks Sam.

"I would like to think I wouldn't," says Mrs. García, "but I know that when you're in a cult, there comes a certain point when you no longer think straight. One author calls that frame of mind 'information disease.'"

"What do you mean by that?" asks Joe.

"What do you say we talk about it over a coke when we get home?"

Later while the three unload groceries, they resume their conversation.

"About this information disease..." Joe begins.

"Yeah, we don't want to catch it," says Sam with a grin.

"And I don't want you to either. Let's say, for example, you're in that cult shooting at the law officers. You weren't always this kind of person. At one time you had control over your own life, but somewhere along the line you lost that control. That actually began right at the beginning when you first met someone who was trying to get you to join the cult, a cult recruiter. You were feeling down or lonely and you were glad to have someone interested in you. You were flattered and had a warm feeling inside. And so when your new 'friend' gets you to talk about your personal life, you talk freely. And when he or she invites you to a gathering of youth, you go willingly."

"*But you're not trapped yet,*" *says Sam.*

"*That's where you're wrong. The noose has been laid, and you have stuck your foot in it. When you give out personal information and don't insist on answers to your questions about the group inviting you, you have stepped into the noose.*"

"*Do you know someone that did that?*" *Sam asks.*

"*You know I got involved that way. And yes, I know a cult exit-counselor, someone who now helps others get free from cults. He says that when he first went to Moonie cult meetings, he did what they asked him to do. He wrote out a lot about his personal feelings. And that information gave the cult leaders power to know how to shape his thinking and behavior for their purposes. If he had understood the power he was handing to them, he wouldn't have cooperated by writing out that information.*"

"*Why can't a person leave later, Mom—after he sees what's happening?*"

"*At those first meetings, you're kept too busy to reflect on what's happening. And when they get you into a suggestible frame of mind, you believe what you hear.*"

"*Yeah, but Sam and I would stick together, and they wouldn't be able to put anything over on us, would they Sam?*"

"*It worked at that lecture we went to,*" *says Sam.*

"*Well, the cult would arrange it so that you two would be separated from each other so that you couldn't compare notes. And besides that, an experienced cult member would stick close to you to make sure you stayed engaged with what's happening. And if you asked too many questions, he or she* would probably try to distract you."

"Yeah, but the shooting part, Mom..." Joe insists.

"I'm getting you to that point. You stop thinking for yourself when you give your will to the group— when you give up your view of the world for the group's viewpoint, once again by your free will."

"You mean everything you do in a cult is by your own free will?" asks Sam.

"So it seems. I call it being kidnapped by choice. After you put your foot in that noose, someone begins to lead you around, but you don't realize that. You think you're doing what you really want to do."

"I still don't see why a person can't leave," says Joe.

"Here's where information plays a big part. The group or cult feeds you with information that makes you afraid to leave. The cult controls you not only by information it gets out of you but by information that it allows you to have. Someone has said that it would be surprising if you didn't believe like a cult when you are cut off from the outside world."

"How can you be cut off?" asks Joe.

"The cult gets you to look to its group for all your needs—mental, emotional, and physcial. You become totally dependent. Sometimes you have to break off old friendships and family ties or, at least, transfer those loyalties to this group. Sometimes you have to give up belongings and finances and go out to to ask for donations. The cult then feeds and houses you and decides what you need. Like many cults, however, mine wasn't a live-in one. Yet like all of them, it plows under your past and builds you a new future within its own narrow and distorted vision."

"Hey, that's totality thinking all right. That's the big yellow bulldozer that Bill calls totality thinking. It plows under everything that makes you who you are," Sam says.

"Is this what brings on information disease, Mom?"

"Yes. After you get shaken loose from your close ties, your beliefs, and your past, the information sorting system of your mind becomes confused and breaks down. Your personality disintegrates. And because you need someone to put your thinking back in order to make sense of the world again, you reach out for help."

"And so the cult comes to your rescue?" asks Sam.

"Yes. The cult that caused the chaos helps you reorganize your personality around its worldview—its view of the world. You are no longer a separate human being; you have become a helpless clone, someone who looks, talks, and acts like everyone else in the group. This information breakdown is 'information disease.' You become dull in awareness and unable to sort and evaluate information. To rehabilitate your thinking, you need help from a deprogrammer or an exit counselor."

"You become a zombie," says Sam. Joe strikes a pose with a mindless, empty stare into space. Then suddenly, he comes out of his zombie condition: "Hey, whatever happened to our cokes?"

"Right here. Help yourselves," says Mrs. García.

A cult member doesn't become a zombie, but one deprogrammer says he recognizes a cult member's mindless state right away. His deprogramming goal becomes to make the mind active again. He probes to find out the lie a person has been programmed to believe, then looks and waits for that moment he can hit upon the one certain point that will drive home the missing truth. Then he pushes and pushes. "When you deprogram people," he says, "you force them to think."

When a person's mind snaps back to normal, the result is like turning on a light in a dark room, the same deprogrammer says. The ex-cult member becomes the individual he (or she) was before he was ensnared; his eyes lose their glassiness, and his facial expression comes alive. Before, as a clone when he looked at you, he would look through you or past you, but now he makes eye contact.

Pam, a former cult member, describes her personality change and then her return to normalcy. She said it was as though she had jumped off a cliff and then later, upon snapping back to her old self, she felt as though she had returned to the place she had left before. "It was like I had gone backwards in my own development, but I knew myself again. It was me, not that other person. How can you explain how it feels to be alive?" she asked.

Not all changes from the cult personality to normalcy are instantaneous; some are more gradual. All, however, require a period for rebuilding the damaged personality.

Why are destructive cults allowed to exist? Because a free country cannot eliminate cults without violating everyone's religious freedom and freedom to assemble. Any group you join voluntarily should have the right to influence you. Therefore, staying free from a cult becomes your responsibility. And remember this: A cult may hide its real name at first. If you are not sure about a group and think it might be all right, you can ask for a person's name and phone number instead of giving out yours, until you find out more.

But cults are not the only destructive engines out there. More and more as time goes by, totality thinking itself is a danger in mainstream life. Wherever you meet a group—in class, in the community, or elsewhere—you can be conditioned to think that group consensus is more important than what you have held dear in the past. And you can be led to break familiar ties and to make the group your confidant, your authority, and your main source of information. And if your support system of family and family friends is weak, you become like clay to be shaped in a group's image—unless you are aware of the possible threat.

You become especially open to this kind of group influence when you experience emotional turmoil and mental confusion or feel cut off from others. To let someone become part of your life becomes a tempting offer—for the desire "to belong" and to be accepted by a group is strong in all of us.

And again, in a free society recognizing a threat is your responsibility. In the community, in the classroom, and everywhere, your defense against this bulldozer kind of thinking is the same as with a cult recruiter—to limit personal information you give out and to insist that groups and instructional programs give open and easy access to manuals and information about themselves. You become a gatekeeper keeping watch over incoming and outgoing information. With this wary approach, no matter how much totality influences multiply, you can meet life with confidence.

Chapter 10

You, the Gatekeeper of Information
Thinking like the times is like dancing with a bulldozer

Sam is learning to be a gatekeeper for incoming influences. Here Bill shows him how the bulldozer of totality-thinking influence digs up moral foundations to make way for radical ideas.

"I'm puzzled," Sam says to Bill. "The Nazis in their death camps didn't just kill people; they played with their minds. The choices they forced them to make don't make sense to me."

Sam and Bill have settled into easy chairs in the professor's living room while Mrs. Updire, preparing dinner, rattles pans in the kitchen. Bill invited Sam over to talk about what Sam has on his mind.

"Give me the specifics," says Bill.

"For example, a mother would have to pick out one of her children to be killed And if she didn't choose one of them, both would be killed. Was this just to be cruel? Is that why they did that?"

"It's cruel all right. A totalitarian system is built on force so leaders in the system are bound to do cruel things. But there is a purpose. The party must control a person totally. And the best way to do that is to force him to take part himself in an evil action. The force they use is a moral dilemma."

"A dilemma is when you have to make a choice and you don't know what to do. Am I right?"

"Yes, a moral dilemma means that whatever you

decide, it's a bad moral choice. Take the mother and her children. She doesn't want either child to die, but the only way she can get one to live is to point at one of them and say, 'Kill that child.' What's she going to do?"

"She has to choose between murder and murder."

"Yes. She has to choose between two evils. Hannah Arendt, an authority on totalitarianism, says the Nazi campaign was an attack on 'the moral person.'"

"So we don't have that kind of thinking here in America, do we, Bill? We haven't gone that far."

"We don't have the action you describe, but we do have the thinking."

"How's that?" Sam asks, as he straightens up in the comfortable chair. "Is it something I might run into?"

"You might. Let me tell you about a survival game at my college. A teacher in training told me about a role-playing game her class learned as an activity to teach to their students. In the game, they had to decide who should survive to repopulate the planet.

"Here's the scenario: The twenty future teachers played the role of themselves as passengers on a spaceship, which had mechanical problems. They had one lifecraft. And since it could hold only seven people, the passengers had to decide who should be saved. They made their decision by each one voting for three survivors who would live and repopulate the planet."

"So which ones did your friend choose to live?"

"She chose three other passengers and left herself out of the lifecraft. That caused quite a flurry. Everyone told her, 'You can't do that.'"

"Why did they get on her?" asks Sam.

"Her instructor said she must have low self-esteem.

And the students thought she was foolish because they couldn't believe someone would choose to do that."

"So how does this game fit in with the mother having to choose between two children?"

"In each case the person faces a moral dilemma."

"And how does the survival game hurt you?"

"For one thing you get so taken up with solving the problem, you don't stop to think about the game's basic premise, or guiding thought," Bill says.

"Let me find the premise... Survival... Repopulate the planet... Some have to die... Oh! Does the premise have something to do with population control?"

"Yes. The premise behind this game is that the earth will be destroyed if too many people live on it, and so controlling population becomes needful. And that can mean getting rid of people, the ones least valued. The way the game is set up, taking human life under certain circumstances is made to seem acceptable. For you're not just choosing the ones who will live; you're choosing the ones who will die."

"Then," Sam says, "just to play the game, you accept its message—even if you don't realize it."

"That's right. To take part in a moral dilemma game, you have to accept the premise."

"At least a game is just a game."

"True. But the thinking processes are the same as in a real situation. Here's how it can affect you, Sam. It makes you question what you believe. It makes you wonder whether you can depend on moral standards to apply in every situation. Before the moral dilemma activity, you considered moral standards to be always reliable. But when that standard fails to help you in the activity, your whole belief system begins to tremble."

"Heavy stuff!"

"Sam, what's the moral belief challenged here?"

"It must be about the value of human life."

"So you say to yourself, 'If I can't depend on the moral truth against murder in all situations, can I depend upon anything as truth?' The experience attacks you as a moral person because it also makes you ask, 'Can I depend upon myself to know what is right or wrong?' And so your moral base begins to crumble."

"You know, Bill, even knowing what that activity is all about, I still feel shaken up thinking about it all. It's all sort of depressing."

"I've got good news, Sam. Remember this. Although the thinking processes in this activity are the same as in real life, the situations themselves are unrealistic. They exist only in the minds of the creators, and they're not accurate. Sure, you'll face difficult dilemmas. That's life. But when you do, the crisis will make you creative enough to rise to the challenge. You'll find a solution you can live with— a right moral choice. The choice may be hard to make because of consequences, but at least you'll know you have the choice to do right."

"Hey, that's a whole new slant—180° different."

"Soup's on—come and get it," Mrs. Updire calls.

"And Sam," says Bill, "aren't you glad program writers don't write the script for your life!"

With Sam, you are learning to be a gatekeeper for *incoming* influences. Now let's see how you can also be a gatekeeper for *outgoing* personal information.

One parent's experience shows how important this

gatekeeping of information can be. Anita Hoge, learned how personal information can be used when she found out her ninth grade son was receiving remedial training—not in math or reading but in attitudes and beliefs. He had given "unacceptable" answers in attitudinal testing.

Attitudinal testing and *inventories* are the most common ways for others to gather personal information about you. Inventories ask direct questions about your personal life. Attitudinal tests gather information indirectly.

Here is what attitudinal testers look for about you:

- ☐ Do you act from your own desires or because of outside influences?
- ☐ How open are you to change?
- ☐ Will you go along with group goals?
- ☐ To what extent will you obey authority figures (parents, teachers, policemen, etc.)?
- ☐ What will cause you to change your behavior or attitudes?
- ☐ What is the center of control in your life? Authority figures, classmates, or yourself?

An attitudinal test doesn't ask direct questions like "What is the center of control in your life?" It asks you what you would do in certain situations and from your answers finds out who is most important to you. By finding out who is important in your life, testers know who influences and exerts some control over you.

In attitudinal testing, you don't know what the test measures or how it evaluates, which means that you may give information that could work against you. The test, for instance, may rate group loyalty higher than you rate independent thinking.

Other channels also influence you while gathering confidential information about you. Two are the school-based clinic and peer counseling. These counselors may play pickup basketball with you. Then if in an informal way, you give personal information to them, you may be referred for further counseling, or you may be influenced toward a value base that accepts sex outside of marriage as all right for teens. My focus is not on the programs themselves but to alert you to be cautious about incoming and outgoing information in any official, investigative setting even if it is informal.

In everyday classroom activity, however, you have more control over what you say and more awareness about what's recorded. And you have the right to see your records. So you can feel free to express yourself—in class discussions, in private talks with teachers, in your writing, in your attitude. This includes journal writing, a common way personal information can be gathered about you. You can welcome this as a time to reflect on what happens day to day and to practice your writing skills. In the classroom you have no reason to hide who you are even if you could.

And although throughout your classroom day, you want to feel free to be yourself, at the same time don't forget that whatever you say, write, or do can become a subject for discussion between teachers, counselors, and other official people. Information gathered can also go into your record either as writing samples or as staff observations and comments. And because of this, you want to give out only information that is not confidential and that will not work against you. As in a court of law, you do not have to testify against yourself or your family.

Chapter 11

Freedom and Totalitarianism
Thinking like the times is like dancing with a bulldozer

Totality thinking reaches its peak in totalitarianism—for there it fully applies its ideas to practical life.

Totalitarianism is a twentieth century invention made possible by technology. Under other tyrants, you have a little privacy and freedom, but under the totalitarianism of Hitlers and Stalins, you have none. Yet their kind cannot conquer worldwide until a new century perfects computer networks. For personal information is the raw stuff of power that feeds totality thinking appetites—power more dangerous than nuclear explosives.

Sam and Denzel compare totalitarian to free:

"Hey, look, Denzel—a computer program, 'Culture, Totalitarian and Free.' Bill and I talked about this."

"And it's interactive, Sam. That's what sounds good to me. I saw this CD ROM for little kids. You just click on a bush and out fly buzzing bees or you click on the windows of the house and the lights go on inside. Or you click on the ocean, and a big whale surfaces."

Sam and Denzel are at a hands-on science museum.

On the computer screen appears a street scene with this subtitle: "This is a street in Country X, a totalitarian country." Then another scene appears: "This is a street in Country Y, a free country. Go back to Country X, the totalitarian country, and look around."

"Click that big outdoor sign, Sam." Sam clicks. The

print enlarges. Sam and Denzel read: "Rules for Living: Love our Motherland... Love the Party... Love the collective... Love your state-assigned job."

"State-assigned job! Love the Party. Love the collective! I'd say the whole thing sounds like state-assigned love, Sam."

"I don't go for that state-assigned stuff either. I'll click the loudspeaker. Listen! Military music. Doesn't that make you want to march? Now look! Everyone's headed toward the community mess hall. That was a powerful click, wasn't it, Denzel?"

"I'll click the bulletin board." Denzel clicks, a crowd parts, and the posted newspaper enlarges.

"Who puts out this paper? There it is: the Party of X. That means this is propaganda, Denzel. Let's go find some news in Country Y."

In country Y, Sam clicks the coin drop of a news vending machine. They hear the coin clang.

"Click the handle to open the door, Denzel." The door falls open. A newspaper unfolds to full view—on one side arguments FOR and on another arguments AGAINST gun control.

The visitors go further down the street of free Country Y. "Click that store, Denzel." A scene inside the shoe store appears. A clerk appears immediately, smiling and asking, "May I help you?" As the clerk brings out shoes to try on, a foot appears on the screen with two hands putting on the athletic shoes. Every time Denzel clicks "no" the clerk goes back and brings out another pair of shoes. When he clicks "goodbye," the clerk smiles and says, "Have a nice day."

"Okay, your turn, Sam. Let's go look for shoes in totalitarian country X."

In X, Sam clicks on a storefront and the inside of the store opens up to an assortment of retail goods. The clerks, talking to each other, ignore customers.

"Maybe we can get some service if you click on the shoes," Denzel says. Sam clicks but nothing happens.

"I'll switch categories, Denzel—from 'experience' to 'encyclopedia' to get information about the countries. Okay, now you choose the subject."

"I'll try 'careers.' Let's see if there's any difference between careers in countries X and Y."

The young men read the following about free country Y: "Business owners, carpenters, artists, news people, professors, ambassadors, street cleaners..."

Then they read this about careers in totalitarian country X: "Carpenters, artists, news people, professors, ambassadors, street cleaners..."

"Something is missing from country X, Denzel."

"I see what it is, Sam. There are no business owners in country X... No business people. Hm... I get it," Denzel says as he pounds Sam. "Of course, there are no business owners in a totalitarian country. The government owns everything."

"Or has complete control of the businesses. Why didn't I think of that, Denzel? Now that you mention it, I guess that's why we didn't get any service at the shoe store in country X. No competition, no service."

No business owners in totalitarian countries! You may be surprised to learn that ownership marks the difference between freedom and slavery. You know the importance of family and the freedoms of speech, assembly, and religion. But you may not fully value the freedom to own property and to buy and sell because property rights do not get the attention they deserve.

Private ownership limits government power. For if government controls what you buy and sell, it controls your survival or death. Private ownership, on the other hand, puts that power in your hands, and it also divides wealth's power among many rather than placing it all in one central government. Also private ownership allows a market system to operate by what is called supply and demand. If people want a lot of particular goods, free enterprise furnishes it; if they don't, free enterprise stops producing it. If supply is short, people will pay more for what they buy. Totalitarian countries, however, lack this market information because they produce things by government command. Therefore, they fall short in producing what is needed, and they also end up with other wasted, unsold goods.

Yet in spite of success and freedom in capitalism, the influence of the times belittles the part business plays in American society. Who is the villain in movies and on television? Is it not the greedy businessman? And is not big business the evil empire?

Of course, wherever there are human beings, there is bound to be some measure of greed and evil, but if government gains control of business, corruption increases because political power encourages abuse more than the rule of law in a free market system. In countries without free markets, the machinery of their daily life functions only when the oil of bribery is applied to it, I learned in my year in China.

There's something else Sam and Denzel wouldn't find in a totalitarian country: Boy Scouts, 4-H, Campfire Girls, Salvation Army, Rotary Club. The only organized activities they would find would be government sponsored ones: political indoctrination meetings, required "volunteer" service, and other activities sponsored by the state's only political party.

The biggest difference between the systems, however, is in the home and and in the place of worship. Because these two havens produce citizens with independent thinking, they threaten the power of the state. Therefore, totalitarian leaders have to shift "the center of control" away from the moms, pops, pastors, and rabbis to the government. Otherwise, power cannot become total.

Then, after the ruling political party replaces the moral authority of the family and organized religion, it sets up a new *social morality*. Everything that supports what the party says is right, and everything that opposes what the party says is wrong. Morality becomes political instead of personal.

A totalitarian country, however, creates a problem for itself. For although it can bulldoze producers of wealth—business owners—and can bulldoze the source of moral goodness—home and worship—it cannot create riches or piety because laws and force have no power to make people good. Without goodness, society cannot be truly free and without freedom, it cannot fully prosper.

Government can only bulldoze. It can destroy morality and freedom, but it cannot create the goodness or wealth a culture needs. Keep this basic truth in mind so that you will be able to recognize an unrealistic philosophy when you see one. For when government promises too much, look out; there's a big yellow bulldozer headed your way.

Chapter 12

A New Authority

Thinking like the times is like dancing with a bulldozer

Totality thinking prepares society for a new authority, which is neither communism nor Nazism, neither left nor right, neither capitalism nor communism, neither conservative nor liberal. It is the radical center. It is center because it is neither left nor right and because it attracts with a middle-of-the-road theme, the environment. And it is radical because it promotes governmental population control. But before we discuss this new authority, let's observe how different people view authority.

Lucas Laubrec sits with schoolboard members in front of one of the microphones. He shakes his head every once in a while to get the hair out of his eyes, and he has the habit of exaggerating his facial expressions. It's like he plays a role but is unsure of his part—yet the role he chooses is to act self-assured.

"Lucas asked me to tell you he was suspended from school for three days for defying authority," the principal tells the schoolboard audience as he introduces the new schoolboard student reporter. "I think Lucas is so honest, he wants me to tell you about his record."

The administrators, board members, and other adults smile knowing smiles at each other. Sam's mother, Mrs. Ming, observes the reactions. "Who are they kidding?" she asks herself. "Lucas so honest?

Can't they see Lucas is proud of the suspension?" She thinks the adults and Lucas are proud of his defiance of adult authority, but no one admits that, of course—especially not the principal introducing the young man. Instead, Lucas is being "honest." And Mrs. Ming asks herself, "Didn't I just see arrogance written on that young man's face?... Or is that my imagination?" She's not sure because Lucas has been otherwise respectful toward the adults.

Sam, a junior, sitting with other band members, has a different reaction. "Way to go, Lucas!" he's thinking. "How come I can't pull off something like that! All I can get glory for is for selling the most tickets to our benefit band concert. Everybody will clap when I stand up and then forget all about what I did. But at school for weeks, everyone will talk about Lucas."

The envy in Sam's thoughts mixes with a little anger aimed at the adults: "If you think Lucas is so great for getting suspended, what do you think about all the work I did? With your mouth, you say I'm supposed to obey all the rules, but you don't really mean it."

Lucas reads the message from the adults the same as Sam. We are proud of your independent thinking, the smiles communicate to him about his suspension. And with this adult influence, his arrogance becomes fortified—although Lucas would be the last to admit that anything or anyone influences his free-wheeling lifestyle.

Sam still struggles with a mixed message from adults in authority, but Lucas, in his defiance seems to enjoy adult favor. Both, however, will have to deal with the "new authority" of the radical center, which is rooted in rebellion.

And because of Lucas's anti-authority attitude, he is the one more likely to be attracted to the radical cause and for that reason to be less likely to investigate its false foundation. But Sam and you can also be deceived by the thinking of the times—unless you develop the hounddog qualities of alertness, ability to sniff out what is hidden, stick-to-itiveness to stay on the trail, courage to face what you find, and willingness to resist. If you make that effort, you'll be able to see through the claims of the radical center.

Its central theme seems to be that overpopulation is the most threatening problem the world faces. This claim has been around since at least 1968 when radical Paul Ehrlich predicted that overpopulation would cause the world to run out of food by 1977. Although no such thing happened, people continue to read Ehrlich's new books and continue *dancing with the bulldozer thinking of the times.*

Scientist Julian Simond was one of those caught up in this dance. Finally, however, when he looked at "facts and statistics," he abandoned the movement. And he's not alone for he's one of many scientists now joining against misleading information.

While alarmists study the shortterm, Simond studies longterm records, which convince him that human welfare improves over the years and will continue to do so for you. While population increased from one billion to five billion over two centuries, your life expectancy overall during that time more than doubled—from thirty years to seventy-five.

Longterm, what did Simond learn about your environment? *Rate* of disappearing species has not increased since the turn of the century. Looking worldwide, not at specific locations, you have no fewer trees on earth now than people had fifty years ago. In spite of increased traffic, pollution has lessened. Your American water and air are getting cleaner, not dirtier.

Longterm social issues? A long history shows a declining murder rate in England—ten times less now than in 1300. In free countries, although the wealth gap between rich and poor has not grown nor decreased, your life whether wealthy or poor has improved. And, Simond says, although hunger, sickness, poverty, war, and pollution strike certain areas, longterm trends under freedom keep improving for you.

And resources? As long ago as 1964, Marshall McLuhan said information power makes possible better use of resources. Time confirms this. Twenty years ago, 165 pounds of aluminum produced 1000 aluminum cans; today, 35 pounds can produce for you the same. A calculator weighed 20 pounds; now you can buy one less than an ounce. Once, raw materials for manufacturing had to be shipped from far away. Now with information, you can create goods on location. And instant communication makes it possible for you to stock less on shelves and in warehouses.

Knowledge power changes everything for you. It decreases labor, space, time, and expense. And energy too can become cheaper. Simond, in fact, goes so far as to say that there is no known limit for taking care of added population. You can go up in the air, under the earth, and under the sea to innovate for living space.

Alarmists, in contrast, base their forecasts on the

theory of increasing scarcity. They overlook the truth that when problems arise, you find solutions. And these solutions offer better living than before your problems. I have seen this principle at work on lesser levels. An expert in the business world observes that businesses with early problems have a better chance for survival. For they don't just survive their problems; they thrive on them. One current author predicts, in fact, that when baby boomers reach their prime, the economy will boom because their numbers make them more competitive. Marriages, too, grow stronger as spouses meet crises and get beyond them. And in personal life, how you meet difficulties determines the quality of your future more than anything else.

The good news is that to have more people is to have *more problem solvers* and better living. Wherever societies allow human beings free rein, progress takes place. But progress won't happen in the world that the radical center would bulldoze and then create. Freedom would disappear. And population control in the form of abortion and euthanasia would usher into positions of world power those who would promote inhumane practices.

In conclusion, think about this. If population had not grown, you wouldn't have electric light or gas heat or autos or penicillin or travel to the moon or your present long-life expectancy. You would be content to grub from berry bush to berry bush.

Chapter 13

FUTURE FREEDOM AND PRESENT THINKING SKILLS
Thinking like the times is like dancing with a bulldozer

Sam, Hannah, Joe, Denzel, and Yolanda learn to apply critical thinking skills in an unusual way:

"I wonder if we're the only high school guys here," Sam says to Joe and Hannah as they watch the crowd gather in the community hall.

"Maybe, but there's more long hair here than at Seabold High," says Joe.

"And definitely more beards," says Hannah.

The conversation ends because the speaker, an author and professor of critical thinking from a nearby university, takes his place before the crowd. His appearance fits the scene—long hair, a football jersey showing through an open sport coat, a scarf dangling long on one end, and scuffed athletic shoes.

Sam, Joe, and Hannah have come to hear him talk about Mid-East problems from a critical thinking viewpoint. "In politics, the media speaks for the right wing," professor Burt begins. "The range of the media runs from near right to far right," The crowd nods agreement. "People in the media debate various shades of the right. Those of us on the left have no real influence... Jesse Jackson is a liberal capitalist. So what happens to the others who are far left or near left?"

"Did you hear that? He puts Jesse Jackson and liberals on the right!" Joe whispers to Hannah.

"The U.S. and England created Stalin," the profes-

sor continues. "They recognized the Soviet Union in 1939, but later treated Stalin as an enemy. Treat someone like an enemy, and he becomes an enemy..." And then later: "A different world is emerging. Let us throw off ignorance and narrow-mindedness."

Every time the speaker ridicules the president of the United States, the audience beams, cheers, or laughs. And when he talks about the medical establishment and education nearing a breakdown crisis, the crowd becomes jubilant. The professor's main topic, however, is about Israel and the Arabs. During that time, Sam notices that Hannah shifts her position a lot; he knows that because she has relatives in Israel, it bothers her to hear anti-Israel talk.

A tall, dark haired man to the right of Hannah, Joe, and Sam begins to speak to the professor: "You're not thinking critically about Israel and the Arabs as you claim. You have a bias against Israel. I'm willing to express and admit my bias: I'm an Israeli citizen. Why don't you admit to this crowd your bias instead of saying you apply critical thinking?" The Israeli then offers facts about Israel and points out inconsistencies in what the professor has said.

Sam watches Hannah brighten and nod as the man speaks. The crowd waits for the professor's defense, but he finds no answer. Instead he moves on.

Later the crowd comes alive when a person says the biggest world problem is neither capitalism nor communism. It's overpopulation. "A good example for environmental excellence is Cuba," she adds. "Environment is a religious issue. The question is, does man have dominion over the Earth?... I think not." The professor agrees.

As Sam, Joe, and Hannah walk out of the hall, they see their African-American friends ahead of them. "Hey, Denzel, Yolanda," Sam calls.

Later as the five of them sit in a booth sipping soft drinks, they talk about their reactions. "How did you feel about the lecture, Hannah?" Yolanda asks.

"I agree with the Israeli," she says.

"What's your reaction?" Sam asks Denzel .

"Same here. That professor didn't have an answer to what that critic said."

"His critical thinking breaks down when the spotlight is on himself," says Yolanda.

Are you alert?

Did you notice a reference to the radical center? The clue for a *radical center* idea is "neither this nor that"—in this case a woman's reference to neither communism nor capitalism, neither left nor right. She attacked the traditional view that human beings have higher status than other species. And she called over-population the world's biggest problem.

Did you wonder why the crowd seemed jubilant to think education and health care approach a state of crisis? Left and right extremists think chaos is necessary to make people willing for radical change.

And did you notice the power of the influence of the real life Israeli? He thrust into the heart of the professor's bias his own tool of critical thinking. And even though the professor and the crowd refused to listen to him, he was willing to stand alone to give them the opportunity to hear the facts.

And in your alertness, check out whatever *appears* to be objective, nonpartisan, or based on good intentions. FIRST, don't assume that an instructor who teaches objectivity is necessarily objective himself. The fact is you are more likely to meet political bias in critical thinking instruction than elsewhere because in this setting, an instructor with a radical bent can bash America or other democracies without fear of criticism. For through an anti-American stance, he (or she) seems to demonstrate openness to other cultures and an ability to rise above his own culture; therefore, he cannot be accused of *ethnocentrism.*

The real life professor in the story, in fact, is the leader of annual international conferences on teaching critical thinking. And his bias is also apparent in the examples and illustrations of the textbook he wrote. Yet in spite of his bent, his book also gives helpful material on critical thinking. When you have no choice, you can learn even from people with an *agenda*—if you stay aware of your *vulnerability* to their powerful influence and seek outside support.

SECOND, don't assume that since instruction in *political activism* seems nonpartisan that you can accept what you learn there without question. You may no doubt find some helpful hints; for instance, an activist manual for teens gives helpful tips on the art of listening:

> Learn to separate ideas from feelings.
> Ask the one talking direct questions.
> Ask why.
> Ask the person to state the idea another way.
> Summarize what the person says and ask if your understanding is correct.

And that same manual says you can use political power to reach your self-interest goals by working with others for their interests. That's okay because that's the way politics works: You join with others in causes that can help you both.

The influence of this manual sponsored by a radical group, however, is very subtle. Mixed in with useful information, the manual defines *everything* in public life as political and says that politics is "the *only* way to work on things that matter to you." And that's a distorted view.

Most political activist instruction for youth leaves out these truths: (a) Politics is not the only way to solve life's problems. (b) All of public life is not political. (c) A career in politics should be a call to statesmanship to serve your country, not a bid for power for yourself or a special interest group.

THIRD, don't assume that an idea is good just because it seems founded on good intentions. The latest trend is to require youth social service. Maryland already requires for high school graduation what some call "mandatory volunteer service." But it is no more voluntary than construction labor by Chinese workers on their only day off. Although encouragement to do volunteer work is good, for government to require that work is to say government knows best how you should serve others. This gives government a foot into another door of your personal life.

In all of this, the totality bulldozer plows under your morals and ideals by convincing you that you do not already own a moral code—your family's—nor belong to a culture—your American culture. Instead of hitting your beliefs head on, the influence of the times pushes you toward a new worldview by making you believe you can't think for yourself unless you reject what family and culture teach. And so you begin to see personal morality as "narrow minded" or "bigoted" and the American way of life as "oppressive."

To offset this influence, face the givens in your life. You can't escape the American or family identity into which you were born. This is who you are. You don't solve your problems by some magical decision to reject your family background or by some mystical power to rise above membership in a culture. Instead, along with the pluses into which you were born, you accept the minuses. Along with benefits into which you were born, you accept responsibilities.

A normal third grader, son of severely mentally retarded parents, accepts the givens in his life—that is, unless he now questions them after an interview on television's Sixty Minutes. Among other scenes, the program showed the boy reading labels for his parents at the grocery store. Later Mike Wallace asked him if he ever wished his parents were different. The youngster frowned and looked at Wallace as though to say what's-with-you, then said, "No, why?" A chastened Wallace commented, "Why indeed?" The boy's teacher said the third-grader is more mature than some his age.

Don't run away from who you are. If you do, you'll run smack into that bulldozer that wants to remake you by first plowing your present identity under its blade.

Are you going to think like the times? Or, like Sam, are you going to find in your private support system and in your culture the bonds that keep you and your country free in spite of the influences of the times?

Chapter 14

LIVING WITH CHANGE
Acting without understanding is like dancing on quicksand

Sam's Senior Year—Chapters 14 - 21—ACTING

Although everyone agrees the world is changing, people disagree about whether truth changes or remains the same, Sam and Cecelia learn.

"You went to Mount Lear's football game Saturday, didn't you, Bill?" Sam asks.

"Sure did. It was a cliffhanger. Wasn't that something how quarterback Mory pulled the team through in the last few minutes?"

Sam and Cecelia chat with Professor Bill Updire in his Mount Lear College office, while the professor waits for one of his students to arrive.

"Did you hear what Mory had to say on the radio after Mount Lear won the game?" asks Sam.

"I heard about it, but what did he say exactly?"

"All he said, Bill, was, 'I'm grateful to know God through Jesus. I thank him for giving me a clear head in a tense moment.' From the way everyone's been talking, you would have thought he did the most awful thing in the world."

"People are angry," says Cecelia.

"Are you surprised?" asks Bill.

"I am. I don't see what their problem is," she says.

"What I don't understand" says Sam, "is why people want to deny Mory his right to free speech."

"That's because free speech has been redefined to

include only what's politically correct," Bill says.

"I see that now. Lots of things get redefined. Before I started paying attention, I missed a lot of what was going on. Looking back I can see that it all went right past me... We do have a question though. Actually, we have a confession."

"Fine. I often play the part of Father Confessor."

"Yeah, we've both been getting together with a bunch of guys at lunchtime... to read the Bible."

"This is serious, isn't it?" Bill teases.

"Our question is, how does the Bible fit into our discussion about objective and progressive truth?"

"You tell me, Sam... but first tell me what you remember about what we talked about before."

"You told us that you see two main worldviews." Sam chuckles, shakes his head as if in disbelief, and goes on: "A while back, if somebody had said I'd be in your office talking about objective and progressive truth, I'd have said they were nuts. But since you explained things to us, one thing happened after another and I began to see how things line up. And you know what? It's sort of exciting to figure it all out."

"Same with me," says Cecelia.

"Anyway," says Sam, "change is the talk of the times. And here's the biggest change—what people say about truth. Until now most people have said truth never changes. But people who believe in progressive truth say truth always changes... Before you go on, Bill, straighten me out on one point. Nobody on the objective truth side objects to progress in general, do they?"

"Of course not. This is so important. They say change in most areas is good, that it's just truth that stays the same. We need progress in technology and science—and in culture and customs, too. All human beings want progress, not just progressive truth people... Cecelia, what can you tell us about worldviews?"

"Well, the two main views find truth in different places. Objective truth people find truth in moral principles outside of themselves, and progressive truth people find truth within themselves or within their group, either in experience or in group consensus—what everyone agrees upon."

"What do you understand about the politics that each worldview seems to favor, Sam?"

"Up to now," Sam says, "objective truth has said society can't be good unless individuals lead good lives, but now progressive truth says individuals can't be good unless society makes them that way. That's a big difference, isn't it, Bill?"

"Yes, I agree. What can you say about the worldviews and morality, Cecelia?"

"The objective side cares about personal character, and the progressive thinks of morality as group involvement—like working for social justice, which, of course, both sides want but in different ways."

"You two really understand what I was talking about. And Sam, you're able to express what you think better than when I first met you. I'm impressed." Sam gives Bill a high five. "I think by next fall you'll both be well equipped to face challenges in college." Sam gives Cecelia a high five. "Cecelia, I think you know what progressive means."

"The word progressive means something gets better," explains Cecelia, "And according to progressive truth seekers, as society improves, people do, too. For instance, our society didn't used to give all adults the right to vote. Now we do. And so progressive truth people see human nature as good and in need only of time to improve more."

"And objective truth people argue with this by pointing at the Holocaust in this century," says Sam.

"Now what does objective truth mean?" asks Bill.

"That's a little harder to explain," says Sam, "but let me try. People who believe in objective truth say that truth exists no matter what you think about it. They say it's out there regardless of what human beings say."

"Close enough, Sam. Maybe you're ready to answer your own question now. Which worldview would you say describes the Bible?"

"Well, it would have to be objective truth because it's about moral principles that never change."

"We understand that, but we have another question," says Cecelia. "If the Bible teaches objective truth, are Christians the only ones who believe in objective truth?"

"What do you think?"

"I don't think so. My parents aren't Christians, but they're always telling me that good has good consequences and evil has evil consequences. We're sort of Buddhists, you know."

"Sort of?" Bill asks.'

"I say 'sort of' because my great grandparents in China combined things from Daoism and Buddhism. But in America, our family goes to the temple just for ethnic gatherings."

"So what's the answer to your question, Cecelia?"

"The answer must be that people besides Christians believe in objective truth," says Cecelia.

"And don't forget, Sam and Cecelia, that Jewish people and Moslems believe in the Ten Commandments. Besides that, all kinds of people believe in objective, unchanging moral standards. And although these people may not always agree about what *is* true, they all agree on one thing—that objective truth does exist."

"All atheists would oppose objective truth though, wouldn't they?" Sam asks.

"Not all of them, Sam. Have you ever heard of Ayn Rand?" Sam and Cecelia shake their heads. "Mid-century, she was a popular intellectual. She wrote The Fountainhead. She was an atheist with an objective truth philosophy. She encouraged everyone to think about philosophy, or worldviews."

"So what you're saying, Bill," says Sam, "is that unchanging personal morality and objective truth go together, but within that view, people have different ideas."

"Yes, Sam. And even people who agree have different reasons for what they believe. Some objective truth people argue their case on what they call 'common sense.' Still others talk about 'natural law' from the Declaration of Independence..."

"And there are a lot of variations on the progressive truth side, too, aren't there?" asks Cecelia.

"You bet... Oh, hi, Ben. Come on in..."

Sam and Cecelia are beginning to understand different views of the world, or different worldviews. They've a lot to learn in days ahead.

Chapter 15

INTEGRATING IDEAS

Acting without understanding is like dancing on quicksand

Today clashing worldviews make it impossible for you to ignore issues. You have to decide how new knowledge fits into your view of the world.

And controversy is what sparked Sam and Cecelia's interest in the Bible. Let's flash back to their first meeting with other students:

At the door ringing the bell stands the blond-haired football player everyone calls Hulk and his new friend, Margaret, a British exchange student. Meanwhile, inside a group of high school students scurry around to put an envelope and some Bibles out of sight. The scene is Joe's house, just across the street from the campus.

"Come in, Hulk, Margaret," Joe tells them when he finally gets to the door.

Students eating from their brown bag lunches exchange friendly greetings between bites. Hulk and Margaret settle on the sofa. A short silence follows. "Well?" Hulk begins.

"Well what?" several ask at once.

"Let's get on with the discussion," Margaret says.

"What do you mean?" Sam asks.

"You know what I mean."

"You mean you know?" asks Carmen.

"Of course, we know. Everyone in school knows you guys are reading the Bible together."

"Oh, no!" They look at each other.

"Now wait a minute," Joe interrupts the implied accusations of exchanged glances. "Isn't this sort of silly—worrying about someone finding out?"

"Yeah, but..." No one wants to admit anything.

"I'm really interested," Margaret says.

"In the Bible? I thought you were an atheist," says Hannah.

"I am an atheist. I'm not interested in the Bible. I'm interested in you guys. In England we don't talk about the meaning of life all the time like you American dudes."

Denzel laughs. "American dudes! Listen to her."

"You mean you're here just to look over us American specimens?" asks Yolanda.

"I want to soak up a little Americana. That's all."

"That's your excuse," says Sam. "Give us time, and the rest of us can come up with good reasons why we're here, too." Muffled laughter follows.

"Yeah, we didn't tell anyone we were meeting because we were afraid we'd get expelled," says Denzel. Loud laughter clears the air.

"Here's what we're up to, Margaret," says Sam. "After what happened to the principal, some of us got curious about the Bible being such a dangerous book. So I got a fact sheet about the Bible."

"Wait a minute. First, tell me what happened to the principal," Margaret says.

"Earlier in the year before you came to our school, the schoolboard told Mr. Washington he couldn't take his Bible with him to the camp on environmental studies."

"He was going to teach the Bible?"

"No, he was going to read privately," says Denzel.

"And so he said he'd resign if he couldn't take his Bible with him," says Cecelia.

"Is reading the Bible illegal?" asks Margaret.

"No," says Cecelia.

"That's why I say he should sue instead of resigning. You know he could," Joe says.

"Of course he could," says Sam, "and he'd win, too. So anyway that incident got some of us wondering why the Bible is so dangerous and why Mr. Washington would care that much, so here we are... Now we're reading this fact sheet, and then we're going to decide on a plan of action for reading the whole Bible together."

"The whole Bible! That will take forever," moans Hulk, an agnostic who came because Margaret did.

"No, it won't," says Sam. "This sheet says it takes only eighty hours to read the Bible out loud. Besides we're going to do most of our reading at home."

"Yeah. Maybe a book a week. The Bible's divided into books, you know," says Joe. "The fact sheet says we don't have to understand it all. We read to get an overview. First we need to find out what a book says and then later each of us can interpret it for ourselves—in our own churches or at home or wherever."

Sam takes time out to see if everyone thinks a book from the Bible every week is a good plan. The group decides to cut long books in half but to read short ones each week. Then they will compare notes to see if they have their facts straight.

"What else does that fact sheet say?" asks Cecelia.

"I thought you'd never ask," says Sam.

"And now I'll take the contents out of its plain

brown-paper wrapping..." Sam looks around furtively. Then with a flourish, he takes a paper out of a white envelope. Everyone laughs. "This fact sheet is for us. Listen: 'A Group Plan for Diverse People Who Want to Investigate the Bible Together.'"

Sam begins reading:

When you read a book, you approach it from the viewpoint from which it presents itself to find out what it's all about. If you read Peter Rabbit, you enter the rabbit world. If you read the Bible, you enter another world. And so to read it in that literary framework, you accept its claim that God is its author and read to find out what that author is like, not only through what he says about himself but by the way he presents his material.

In this case, the author doesn't dwell on theory. According to the Bible, he presents a record of his dealings with individuals and groups of people. Bible scholars say he presents his story through Jewish writers except for one Greek writer, all of whom did their writing over a period of about 1500 or 1600 years, according to some estimates.

This is the approach by which your diverse group can unite to read the Bible—to find out the message and character of the one author that the Bible claims. Whether in belief, disbelief, curiosity, or for cultural enhancement, you read to find out the contents. This first fast reading will give you familiarity with the material. Several fast readings will be necessary to get a better overview of the biblical panorama.

"This is real subversive stuff, Sam," says Joe.

"Don't interrupt, Joe," his friend Carmen tells him. "I don't know anything about the Bible."

"I like this tack," says Margaret. "Keep reading."

Sam continues:

Most of the Bible is written in two classical languages, Hebrew and Greek, but it also has a few short passages in Aramaic. Although modern day Hebrew and Greek are living, changing languages, the classical Hebrew and Greek of the Bible are dead languages, no longer in active use and frozen in time, with meanings that have not changed over the years. Therefore, scholars are able to compare passage with passage to get meanings that have not been corrupted by time..."

"I'm learning something, too," says Denzel, "and I've heard a lot of reading from the Bible."

"We're going to have to break this up, or we'll be late for class," says Sam. "Read the first half of Genesis. See you next week. Same time. Same place."

"And get an easy Bible to read," says Denzel as the students make their way out.

"Wait until Lucas Lautrec finds out what we're doing," says Joe. "He's going to make hay with this."

"If he makes hay," says Hulk, making a fist as he follows Margaret out. "I'll give him something to make it with—a haymaker! Nobody's going to hassle me."

Hostility toward the Bible arouses curiosity. Students wonder why anyone would worry about what a principal reads in his free time. Such controversy sparks investigation because when viewpoints clash, worldviews matter.

And you live in just such times—worldview-promoting times that cause heated controversy. Flooded with information from opposite directions, you feel the need to make sense of it all. And so to adjust to a changing world, you reexamine assumptions and sort out personal preference from principle. That's how you integrate, or weave, knowledge into your worldview.

And just as you as an individual feel the need to integrate what you learn, educators want to help you integrate subjects under broad unifying themes. This will not be a problem for you with topics that give you room to take them where you will—such topics as, observations, patterns, light, humor, flight, pioneers, the future, student life, current events, historical events. But in a high school program like Humanitas, you are more likely to run into a point of view being promoted by material available. There you choose between such topics as "Women, Race, and Social Protest" or "The Protestant Ethic and the Spirit of Capitalism."

In this kind of program, after you finish each unit, you must write an essay based on questions that bring together what you've learned in all your related classes. For instance, if you're a ninth grader who studied "Culture and Traditional Societies," you could meet this typical exam question: "The cosmology of a traditional culture permeates every aspect of that culture. This is illustrated in the following three cultural groups: the Eskimos, the Southwest Indians, and the Meso-Americans. Specifically, discuss the spirit world that each group believed in, and explain how it influenced their culture and values. Include examples from your reading in art history, literature, and social institutions to illustrate and substantiate your analysis. Finally, to what extent, if any, does the spirit world affect us today?"

Or later when you go to a public or private university, you may come across team teaching—for example, a mathematician, an astrophysicist, a biologist, and a geologist with a philosopher, theologian or anthropologist. The subject might be something like "Introduction to the Cosmos," says Vartan Gregorian, president of Brown University. He says that students could explore such questions as these: "What are theories about the universe? Are we alone in the universe? What happens if humanlike creatures are discovered on Mars? Are they made in the image of God? Has Christ risen for them, or for us only? What are the theological issues about not being unique in the universe?"

These examples of integrated studies show you that in the emerging world, whether you want to choose a worldview or not, you will meet influences of the times that organize learning around basic ideas. You have no choice but to integrate into your life what you see, experience, and learn. And in so doing, you will be influenced toward the principles of some worldview. Your choice is whether you swallow whole whatever is presented to you or whether you become aware of subtle influences.

Truly, these are worldview-promoting times, in which *acting without understanding is like dancing on quicksand.* And that's the topic of the next chapter— the pull of totality thinking quicksand.

Chapter 16

Resisting Harm
Acting without understanding is like dancing on quicksand

Unless you understand the times, the deceiving quicksand of a totality thinking worldview can politicize you. Sam alerts his cousins to some hidden hazards.

"We're coming to an intersection," says Sam. He is walking beside a paved road with his cousins—Robert, a second grader, and Pam, a fourth grader. "There's a danger here you might not think about. You have to watch for cars coming around the corner."

While they wait for the traffic light to change, Sam warns his cousins: "When you walk, you feel safer than you are. I know what I'm talking about because before I started driving, I felt safe walking."

"What do you mean, Sam?" Robert wants to know.

"Well, when I'm driving now, pedestrians come out from behind parked cars, and I almost hit them. Or sometimes people walk on the edge of the pavement and I have to swerve to miss them. When I used to walk and do things like that, I felt safe."

After the three cross over, Pam asks, "Speaking of danger, Sam, can you tell us about quicksand? My mom told me that there is some around here outside of town,"

"Yeah, tell us, Sam," says Robert, his eyes getting bigger. "Can it swallow you alive?"

"Some quicksand can. When we get back to the house, you can look it up in our new encyclopedias."

"*Just tell us what they say, Sam,*" Robert begs.

"*Fortunately for you, I happened to look this up. You know why? When my mom bought these encyclopedias, a couple of my mom's friends and a couple of mine came over. And we all sat around and read and looked at the pictures. It was fun—like a party almost. Anyway, I read about quicksand. It's fine sand, and when it's dry, it looks like powder. That's not when it's dangerous though. It's dangerous when water forces itself up through the sand and makes the grains swell and makes the sand lose its firmness.*"

"*So then when you step on it, it can't hold you.*" says Pam.

"*So what do you do if you step on it by mistake?*" Robert wants to know.

"*You don't want to struggle or you'll go deeper. So, whatever you do, don't panic. Stay calm, Robert.*"

"*I don't know if I could,*" says Robert, his lower lip quavering.

"*Sure you can if you know what to do.*"

"*Come on, tell us, Sam.*"

"*You fall flat on your back with your arms out like this.*" Sam holds his arms out at right angles to his body. "*And you float on the sand.*" Robert holds out his arms, too.

"*Like you float on water?*" asks Pam.

"*Yes, with your weight evenly distributed, you just relax.*"

"*But you can't stay there forever,*" says Robert, still holding out his arms.

"*Here's what you do. Ever so slowly you roll over to solid ground,*" Sam says as he turns around *several times in slow motion. Robert copies Sam's turning. "And then you're free!" shouts Sam, raising both arms in victory.*

Robert throws his arms up, too. "Wait 'til I tell the kids at school!"

When Robert and Pam walk down a road, they feel safer than they really are. That's the way it is with you in a world that has harmful influences. If you have no personal moral code to hang on to, no understanding of the basics of your culture, and no clear worldview, what's to keep you from accepting without question everything you hear? Then in the quicksand of totality thinking, you'll surrender to a power greater than your own.

And even if you understand totality thinking, the pull is strong. That's what one man found out. After he had rescued his own son from a destructive cult, he returned to investigate it as an outsider. Yet in spite of his knowledge and expertise in the field, he couldn't stay the full week; he had to leave after three days. So strong was the downward pull that he says that if he had stayed only six hours longer, he would have become one of them; he'd have gone under himself. He felt the pull of the quicksand of cults.

"You can feel it coming on," he says. "You start doubting yourself. You start to question everything you believe in. Then you find yourself saying and doing the same things they are. You feel like you're sinking in sand, drowning—sometimes you get dizzy." When the man saw he was about to become a cult clone, he fled. And only because he is a cult expert was he lucky enough to escape—but barely.

The downward pull of political quicksand is strong, too. Radical activists set up a situation that forces you to choose sides. And by polarizing you this way, they pull you into their political power play.

When protesters shut down a bridge that connects parts of a city, people say, "This could keep somebody from getting to a hospital. Don't the protesters know they make people mad and turn them against their point of view?" Yes, they know. But by throwing mass tantrums, radicals get you involved politically whether you want to or not. The more you fight, the more you spiral into their scheme. For by making you look foolish, radicals turn your opposition to their advantage. Your anger gets attention for their issue and launches their campaign for power.

If you fight the pull of political quicksand, you go under faster the more you struggle. On the other hand, if you just stand in place passive and neutral, you go under just the same, even if not quite as fast. Either way you become politicized, or involved in their politics. So what can you do to keep from being swallowed up? Understand the group's objective: Its members want to control your action.

Refuse to play their game. Handle political quicksand like physical quicksand: Lean back, relax, and float on top of the situation. Then roll yourself ever so slowly to solid ground the way Sam advised his cousins. From that perspective, you can evaluate the situation with reason, commonsense, and without spite. You can act politically in wisdom your way—but only if you prepare yourself to understand worldview-promoting times.

Chapter 17

Your Total Environment
Acting without understanding is like dancing on quicksand

A totality thinking worldview is *comprehensive:* It works through the total environment to reshape you as a whole person—mind, body, emotions, and spirit.

Bill Updire, Sam, Joe, and Denzel meet in Joe's living room to listen to the introduction of a tape that Joe's mother ordered—a *spiritual* workshop for public school teachers. This is what they hear:

Good evening. My name is John Doe. I am superintendent of the Good Public School District." (Bill looks surprised when he recognizes the superintendent's voice.)

Let me speak from my heart. Two women from Against War asked the school district to co-sponsor this workshop... Then after we heard preview tapes of Sister Miriam MacGillis we were not only willing, we were ready to knock down the doors to be part of this weekend teacher workshop. And our board of education voted a formal co-sponsorship of this event." ("Did you hear that Bill?" Sam asks.)

These are confusing, bewildering, frightening times. It is Sister Miriam's gift as a teacher, as a person of faith, to provide a context for understanding and a ray to shine in our hearts... ("Does that sound like religion or what?" Joe asks.) Listen to the inspired words of our sister.

After the group finishes listening to the intro-duction, Sam says, "We listened to all the tapes, and I can sum up both days of the workshop." Everyone looks at Sam. "The Earth is mother of all."

"He's right. It was like nothing I'd ever heard before," says Denzel.

"Did she call her ideas a cosmology?" Bill asks.

"Yes," the three young men answer at once.

"She has this thing about the Delaware Indians," says Sam. "She says there are three scriptures: Earth, Delaware Indians, and all religions."

"She compares the Delaware Indians and the an-cient Celtic church," adds Joe.

"Those are two things you will hear about a lot in the future," says Bill, "—the Celtic and Native American religions. These are pagan religions that worship many gods. They are closely connected to nature and the earth," explains Bill.

"Do you know what she said, Bill?" asks Denzel. "The Delawares believe the Great Spirit lives inside the earth. And because the Great Spirit lives in the earth, all creatures on the earth live. If the elk breathes, the elk breathes through the earth. The elk reflects the earth. This was their science."

"She said something else about the Delaware In-dians," says Sam. "You know how scientists finally learned to split the atom and that made possible the atom bomb? She said the Delawares would never split the atom because they would never 'open the Mother.' That's what she said. I kid you not."

"Yeah, she made us look sort of dumb," Joe adds. "She said the Delawares already knew what was in-side the atom because they could see it from a spir-

itual view just by going into a trance. And she said they didn't have to crawl into a machine to find out the secrets of the universe."

"And what did Sister Miriam say about the relationship between human beings and the earth?"

"That was her main point," says Sam. "The human is the being through which the earth becomes conscious of itself. It's because of us that the earth now can think, understand, remember, and choose."

"She makes it sound pretty awesome," says Joe. "She says that with our knowledge about technology, we have power over the physical energies of the planet—so much so that we are taking the earth off the automatic system it's been operating on without our help for fifteen billion years."

Sam explains: "So that means that the earth knows only as much as we know. If we don't know, it doesn't know."

"Hey, in that case, we'd better go home and hit the books right now," Denzel jokes.

"No, we can stay a few more minutes," says Joe. "Sister Miriam says we belong to a transition class that will last about twenty years."

"So what are those twenty years supposed to be like?" asks Bill.

"Full of stress," says Joe "because almost all our institutions are rooted in the old cosmology."

"Yes, all our politics, medicine, and economy," says Sam.

"So we live in the old cosmology while we're thinking new cosmology, and we have a hard time pulling the two together," Joe finishes.

"Then after the transition period," says Sam,

"the next evolution takes place. That's when we learn to tap into the memory written in our genes."

"Yeah, according to what Sister Miriam said, I'll remember when I lived in the deep seas," says Joe.

"And when I lived in the sun," says Denzel.

"And when I remember the very beginning," says Sam. "I can remember the beginning because the universe within me remembers."

"Hey, guys, are you putting me on?" Bill asks.

"No," says Denzel. "She really said these things."

"You should have heard the clapping," says Sam.

"What did she say about death?" Bill asks.

"She says one animal eats another animal," says Denzel. "So it dies into life. Everything in nature feeds something else; they die into life. We're the only ones that want to die out of life, she says."

"Since this workshop was for teachers, what did Sister Miriam say about education?" Bill asks.

"Listen to what I wrote down, Bill," Denzel says. "'What the child thinks and feels must be revered whether it's right or wrong,' Maybe I can convince Mrs. Stout about that on my next test."

"Don't count on it, Denzel," says Joe.

"Sister Miriam also said the curriculum is not most important," says Sam, "that process is what matters. What did she mean by that, Bill?"

"She was describing, the new trend in education to emphasize not what you learn but how you learn. Content becomes unimportant... Did she talk about a radical center?"

"I never would have noticed a radical center," says Sam, "if you hadn't talked about it to me. Sister Miriam says that fundamentalists and liberals claim *to have the truth, but she sees something beyond both of those viewpoints. I wrote down what she said: 'Communism and capitalism are shadow sides of each other. We need to integrate both.'"*

"And what will make that possible?" Bill asks. "What will tie them together in a radical center?"

The three confer briefly and say "The earth!"

Sister Miriam's education teaches the whole child in his or her whole environment. The concept of her education is *comprehensive* and its spiritual heartbeat, pagan earth religion.

The trend in education and government is to be comprehensive. Up to the present, community life in America centers in private activities engaged in by personal choice. The trend, however, is to try to improve community life through comprehensive government services—with health, welfare, daycare, tutoring, elderly services, after-school activities, recreation, adult education, and other services offered on a school campus or in some neighborhood location. Sounds good, doesn't it? But that's how you become dependent on government. And when you become dependent on government, you end up being controlled by it, too.

And so, as the total environment becomes politicized and narrows its focus on the worldview of the times, it excludes what generations once treasured as ideals. If you, however, become aware that another worldview exists, then you have an alternative—to seek other influence and support. And don't forget that you still have rights even as a student to think, to speak, and to write. You can be an influence.

Chapter 18

A NEW PREJUDICE
Acting without understanding is like dancing on quicksand

A totality thinking worldview requires a common enemy against which a group or groups can unite, Denzel finds out. He faces prejudice of a different kind:

In Sam's backyard, Bill Updire sits on a saw horse while Joe and Denzel sit on the back steps and Sam leans against the house.

"What is a fundamentalist, Bill?" Sam asks. He, Joe, and Denzel wait for an answer.

"Why do you ask?"

"On that teachers' workshop tape, Sister Miriam said that a couple—friends of hers—had experienced several disasters, and one disaster was that two of their children had married fundamentalists."

"So what is a fundamentalist, Bill?" Joe asks.

"Who knows?" Bill answers.

"Hey, we thought you'd know," Joe says.

"Some people who use the term accuse American fundamentalists of being like the fundamentalists in the Near East, the ones who terrorize because of their intolerant beliefs. So what a speaker usually means to imply is that a fundamentalist is narrow-minded, bigoted, misguided, and dangerous."

"But, Bill, these people call Christians that name—fundamentalists!" exclaims Denzel.

"Let's take the term 'fundamentalist' by itself. What it means is one who believes in the basics of

a system of ideas. So it makes a lot of difference which set of fundamentals someone refers to. You can refer to the fundamentals of physics, for instance—or to the fundamentals of basketball. So, when fundamentalist is used in the Christian context, that would mean a Christian who believes in the basics of the faith as found in the Bible. In practical application, however, people have twisted the meaning to change it to mean someone who interprets the Bible in absurd ways."

"Why do they do that?" asks Sam. "I thought Christians were supposed to be nice sort of people."

"Some people oppose the American outlook of the past two centuries, and so they attack people with those values by calling them fundamentalists. Totality thinkers, you see, need an enemy to unite them."

"Yeah, but don't some people really have absurd interpretations of the Bible, Bill?" Sam asks as he picks up his cat and strokes her.

"Of course, at least according to the viewpoint of some people. But that's no reason to ridicule anyone..." Bill stands up. "Say, guys! Don't you have Friday off because of teacher in-service meetings?"

"We sure do. Why?" asks Joe.

"The college is having a free lecture open to the public at noon Friday. You see, I have a suspicion the lecture is going to be against fundamentalists. And I think it's going to be an eye opener."

"What's the topic?" asks Denzel.

"The news article says the lecture will be about the theology of family battering."

"Sounds strange. What makes you think the lec-

ture is about fundamentalists?" asks Joe.

"A hunch, I guess you'd say."

On Friday, the four friends seat themselves near the front of the tiered lecture hall, which is filling up fast. The speaker, Leota Foster, is introduced as a minister of a mainline denomination. (Here is her actual real life speech in condensed form:)

I am not here as a service provider, a scholar, or a theologian but as a survivor of this kind of violence...

Wife-battering follows a pattern: Tension builds, the husband beats his wife, and then he makes excuses. His violence will be worse next time.

This kind of man is rarely violent outside the home. My father, while a doctor in the Navy in Korea, used uppers and downers. When I was six he returned home addicted but denied his addiction; the Navy denied it; everyone denied it. My mother went through four years of hell, and no one intervened. Finally, she left my father. She would have left sooner if she had known that eventually he would attack me.

My mother had guts. *[Foster stopped, looked down, as though she could not go on.]* She left my father, became a secretary, saved pennies, entered a university as a thirty-four year old, probably the first at that age at that time. Later she remarried to a clergyman. Together they told me not to tell any of the good church people that I had a birth father still living, so I entered the conspiracy of silence. If we hadn't done that, people would have turned away from us.

Why do good Christian people turn the other way? They believe that the Bible teaches that wives are inferior to husbands. The Bible is a library of many books, but all the writers are male and speak of women as property... Religion teaches that abusive relationships are natural and morally just. In a patriarchal Christian universe, the wife becomes the chosen victim...

How did Jesus die? He was crucified.

Why did he die? To redeem the world.

What did God have to do with his death? He sent Jesus. Isn't that a violent way to act—to *send* his son?

Batterer and battered follow this model. People believe a love-atonement has life-changing power in their situation; that is, they think the woman's sacrifice will make up for the man's wrongdoing. Men and women are not helped by the religious story line...

"Onward Christian Soldiers, marching as to war" is a Christian song. It upholds the Crusades, the unjust inquisition, organized massacres, the Ku Klux Klan, and Vietnam. Christians think they are saved by violence, by the blood atonement...

Does religion cause family violence? No, it doesn't have to. You can read the Bible in a way that liberates you. You need to see that Jesus' death was political, that he was crucified by the Romans—the ones in political power. Radical theologian Matthew Fox gave up "blood theology" because he says it is a teaching made up in recent history. He traces great thinkers through the Hebrews, through Jesus to Meister Eckert, Adrienne Rich, the Sufi Moslems, Native Americans, WICCA, Zen, Africans, and branches of Judaism.

At present, the world has one religion—a patriarchal, man-centered, and violent one...

Afterwards, the audience claps with enthusiasm.

As the four walk to Bill's car, Sam, Denzel, and Joe talk all at once, but Denzel, the most excited, breaks through the noise barrier: "Bill! You've got to listen. I can't believe what that speaker said. If my family could have heard that, they would have dropped over dead. They would be shocked."

"My folks would have been shocked, too," says Joe.

"What about you, Bill?" asks Sam. "Did you ever hear anything like that before?"

"No, fellows, this is something new. I think we witnessed the first volley of a campaign that you can expect to get in full swing through the nineties."

"What were some of the things that got to you the most, Denzel?" Sam asks.

"When she started ridiculing the blood atonement and calling Christianity a blood religion. It was bad enough that she attacked. But besides that, she didn't have anything right."

"That went over my head," says Sam. "What did she say that was inaccurate?"

"I don't know. I can't think. Help me out, Bill," says Denzel.

"You're right, Denzel. She was on the attack, appealing to people's emotions and distorting facts."

"Like what, Bill?" Sam persists.

"She started off by throwing aside her titles and

presenting herself as a survivor. That was one way to play on people's heartstrings."

"And when she talked about her father's abuse and how heroic her mother was, she choked up and had to stop," says Joe.

"So it seemed," says Bill. "She said that religion teaches that abusive relationships are natural and morally just because the wife has done something for which she must sacrifice herself. I never heard anything like that from any theologians I know."

"And she said the blood atonement was added years later. What about that, Bill?" Denzel asks.

"That's not true. You find atonement in scripture itself, including Hebrew scripture."

"What was that about 'Onward Christian Soldiers?'" asks Joe. "We don't sing that hymn in my church, but I have heard it. Is that talking about Christians going to war, like in the Crusades?"

Bill laughs. "You'd think so from what Leota Foster said."

"The war in the song is spiritual warfare, isn't it, Bill?" Denzel asks.

"That's the idea. It has nothing to do with war except as a picture of fighting evil, not people."

"Hey, Bill. You were wrong when you said she'd talk about fundamentalists," Sam says.

"You're right. She didn't use the word. But ask Denzel if she didn't hit on the basics of the faith," Bill says.

"Yeah, man! She sure did," answers Denzel.

"It is significant," Bill says, "that she talked not about fundamentalists but about Christians because she's a step ahead of everyone else. She's already dropping the adjective fundamentalists and talking about Christians. This public lecture breaks ground that hasn't been touched before."

"Bill, is it true that the Bible says that women are just property?" Sam asks.

"You guys are reading the Bible. Have you come across anything like that?"

"No."

"Well, keep reading. You won't find anything like that. The Jewish people and Christians exalt womanhood above other cultures... Here's my car. Climb in."

"There's something I don't understand, Bill," says Denzel.

"What's that?"

"What gives a person the right to attack my faith?" asks Denzel.

"Free speech," says Sam.

"I know about racial prejudice. This prejudice is a new one," Denzel says as he shakes his head.

"Where to?" Bill asks.

"McDonald's."

"Burger King."

"Jack in the Box."

"I'll break the log jam. We'll go to Wendy's," says Bill as he starts the motor.

Chapter 19

WORLDVIEWS IN CONFLICT

Acting without understanding is like dancing on quicksand

Worldviews clash in basic ways, Sam learns. They disagree about authority, standards, regard for human life, and the meaning of tolerance and pluralism.

Bill has invited Sam to his home office to discuss material for a book he's writing for young adults.

To review, Bill asks Sam the main difference between the worldviews. "Objective says truth doesn't change; progressive says truth always changes," Sam responds as he dips into the popcorn bowl between him and Bill.

"Here's something new," Bill says. "Objective truth separates things—into an inner and outer person, into an individual separate from the outside world, and into the material world separate from the spiritual, but it sees each part as interactive with the other. Progressive truth, on the other hand, sees the oneness of all things."

"Too complicated. Can you draw me a picture?"

"Okay. I see the objective truth individual as two circles," Bill draws two circles. "That's two separate circles. And to show that the inner and outer life of a person interact with each other, I link the two circles." Bill draws two circles interlinked. "That's the picture of an individual—a two part or three part person according to how you look at the linked circles. But for our purposes here, we care

only about the two parts. Now I'll place that person in the material world." Bill draws a circle around the linked circles. "Inside the big circle is the material world, and outside the big circle is the spiritual world...Now, drawing the progressive truth view is easy." Bill draws a single circle.

"That's it?"

"That's it."

Sam studies the diagrams.

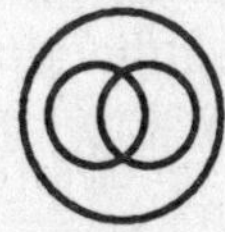 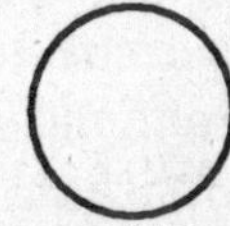

"So, in progressive truth, is the spiritual world outside that single circle?"

"No, everything is all right there inside the circle—the inner and the outer person, and the person and the outside world, and the material and the spiritual worlds."

"And didn't you say progressive truth has people with a lot of different ideas just like objective truth does?"

"That's true. There are a lot of single circle worldviews," Bill says between popcorn bites. "There's New Age, humanism, and paganism—to name a few. They put different ideas inside their circles, but they see the world through the same lens."

"How can that be?" asks Sam.

"Each one says 'All is something.' They just have different somethings."

"Isn't that totality thinking? Tell me more."

Bill draws three circles. "Humanism says, 'Human interaction is the measure of ALL,'" he says while he writes the sentence inside one circle.

"So humanism is mostly about relationships?"

"Yes, Sam. Then there's New Age. It says 'ALL is one and one is ALL,'" Bill says while he writes that sentence in another circle. "Someone who meditates says he experiences the oneness of all things."

"What about paganism?"

"It says, 'Earth is mother of ALL'" says Bill as he fills in the third circle.

Sam frowns. "How does this help me, Bill?"

"Now we've come to the important part, Sam. When you live out one worldview or another, things come out differently."

"Is that when worldviews clash?" Sam asks.

"Yes, they collide as you live out a worldview in your religion, politics, conduct, and lifestyle."

"I don't think my friends sit around strategizing about their worldview."

"No, but they live according to one worldview or another even if they don't consciously choose one."

"So how do worldviews come out differently?"

"For one thing," Bill says, "each has a different authority, a different center of control. For instance, tradition says there are unchanging personal moral principles by which to live, principles that we ourselves don't make up."

"Bill, you can't believe principles are unchanging and lasting unless you believe an unchanging being set them up."

"That seems to be implied, doesn't it?" says Bill. "On the other hand, one circle people believe moral standards progress. And if they refer to a god at all, they don't see him as separate from themselves and

their world nor as their authority. So in their personal lives, he becomes meaningless and irrelevant."

"Authority is a key word in all this, isn't it?" Sam asks before he throws a popcorn kernel in the air and catches it in his open mouth. "Oops, I forgot. I don't want to mess up your office."

"You lucked out because you caught it... Yes, authority is key. Progressive truth people encourage you to question authority."

"Wait a minute, Bill. There seems to be a contradiction here. Objective truth people seem to be the ones swimming against the tide and questioning what's happening even under adult leadership. Aren't they also saying to question authority?"

"Let me explain. Objective truth is the traditional view of our culture. Progressive truth is anti-tradition; that's why we call it counter-culture. Our traditional culture respects authority, but the counter-culture questions whether authority has even the right to exist."

"But when objective truth says to question what's going on, isn't that saying to question authority?"

"Sam, the difference is that you can raise questions and challenge situations and still respect the office someone holds. It's a matter of tolerance. You give others the right to express themselves, and you expect to have the same right."

"Is there a difference in the way these worldviews look at us human beings?" Sam asks.

"This difference marks a big divide. Traditionalists believe human life is sacred. One-circle people deny this."

"Wait a minute. What about humanism? That

viewpoint respects human life, doesn't it?"

"It might look that way, but no, that's not true. There are all kinds of humanists, but practically speaking, humanists endlessly search for meaning without expecting to find anything higher than their own thoughts. The value they place on human life is not sacred because they regard it only on a human level."

"What about New Age? People into that are big on improving self-esteem—and humanists are, too. Isn't that valuing human life?"

"Far from it, Sam. To believe in the unity of all life puts gods, people, and all things on an equal plane. So, although human life may be called sacred, in reality it is no more sacred than the life of another species—or a rose or a stone."

"Hmm..." Sam stops to think. "Bill, you realize, don't you, that I don't know much about humanism or New Age. Aren't you getting ahead of me?"

"No, Sam. I'm giving you what you need right now to see basic differences in the big picture."

"What I want to know more about is the real world—like how can we all best live together?"

"Well, so far under our traditional worldview in our American society, we have been able to live with tolerance for differences."

"But Bill, opponents of traditional people are the ones who preach tolerance and who accuse traditionalists of wanting to force their views on society."

"There's confusion about what tolerance means, Sam. In its traditional and its dictionary meaning, tolerance means allowing beliefs or practices different from your own. It doesn't mean your acceptance, endorsement, belief in, or support of all other views."

"Hm," says Sam. "Redefining tolerance is another case of making up new definitions for old terms. Still I have to think about that... But how about this? Even though Americans have always stressed tolerance, we have had conflict in our history."

"Of course. In every society there is conflict. The conflict today, however, is different from the past. You hear a lot about pluralism and diversity—about having a society with a lot of different ethnic groups and lifestyles. Well, this new pluralism focuses on social groups and not on people as Americans, and so it tends to divide. But that's not the real problem. The real problem is that the conflict today is not within the system but against it by radicals who want to replace it."

"That's a basic conflict, Bill."

"You're so right." Bill closes his notebook. "Next time when we look at my reality chart, we'll investigate this further."

Chapter 20

LOOKING FOR CORE BELIEFS
Acting without understanding is like dancing on quicksand

Even if the core beliefs of a worldview are extreme, people with a wide range of ideas may support it, Sam learns.

And he learns something about himself.

"Here I am. Show me the reality chart, Bill."

"Are you eager or what?"

Sam takes time out to study the chart. Finally he tells Bill, "I couldn't have done better myself."

"Well, thank you, Sam."

"We've already talked about the worldviews except for a few things about the counter-culture, or progressive truth people. You haven't said much about 'Process is more important than content.'"

"Sister Miriam talked about that. Remember? And I gave you education's popular saying, 'Learning how to learn is more important than what you learn.'"

"There's some truth in that, isn't there, Bill?"

"Yes, of course, but only to a degree; otherwise content becomes unimportant, and that's not good because content is important if you are to excel. For excellence doesn't happen accidentally; you have to aim for it to achieve it... And the other statement on the chart, Sam—'What works is more important than principle'—that's untrue because to give up principle is to give up what makes life worth living."

"But Bill! Progressive truth has to choose 'what

works' over 'principle' because if truth changes, then you can't have any principles to live by."

"Good thinking, Sam. With progressive truth, you have no principle to guide you except the principle that change is all you can count on."

"Bill, how did you come to these conclusions?"

"Well first, experience had to wake me up."

"What kind of experience?"

"An experience with my closest friend showed me the nature of progressive truth thinking. I supported him through an ordeal under the ministry of a radical-theology pastor. That got my attention. And what I've learned since then about totality thinking makes me willing to take a stand against it.

"Now as to how I come to my conclusions... Usually I start with a question in my mind. I pay attention to ideas I come across, then shuffle them to look for patterns. And I follow up my hunches to see if evidence supports them. Things aren't laid out neatly for me to see through what's going on, but after I figure out what's happening, facts are on my side."

"Some New Age and humanist stuff sounds far out to me, but some of it sounds okay. What about that?"

"There's a wide range of beliefs in humanism and in New Age," says Bill. "So you have to look for their core beliefs. The official core belief of humanism is atheism, as you see in Humanist Manifestos I and II, but not all humanists believe that. Some call themselves theists, or believers in God."

"So humanist ideas cover a wide range," says Sam.

"Also under humanism there's humanistic psychology, Sam. You can learn a lot about behavior from those who study it. Humanistic psychology gives a higher view of humanity than earlier psychology. And the ideas seem helpful in the clinic, even if they can do harm in the general classroom."

"Do New Age people disagree about things, too?"

"Yes, Sam, there's a whole spectrum. But again, the core belief itself is extreme. In fact, bookstores used to label New Age books 'occult.' Yet some of what has been called New Age is nothing more than positive thinking. That's why I say that within the counter-culture movement, there is a wide range of ideas that people believe."

"New Age is occult. What is occult exactly, Bill?"

"It's belief in the supernatural apart from the creator God... And, Sam, according to a friend who owns a bookstore, we're now in a new phase. New Age books won't be shelved as New Age or occult because they'll be shelved throughout the store. My friend says that since the term New Age fell out of favor and since New Age ideas went mainstream, New Age books appear under many popular headings."

"Bill, that means people will be influenced by a worldview without realizing it."

"It happens all the time," says Bill. "And here's another trend. In New Age, Eastern religion is giving way to folk religion. What's 'in' now are Celtic religion, WICCA, or witchcraft, Native American shamanism, and goddesses from many cultures.

"And Sam, a school librarian told me that books about religions of other cultures are popular in the classroom. That's because folk religions and folk tales from other cultures fit right into multicultural literature, into integrated studies with topics like anthropology, and into comprehensive education that teaches the whole person. Then, of course, earth religion is part of the environmental message while goddesses are favorites of feminist literature. So the female earth goddess Gaia receives a lot of attention these days. On the chart you find her listed next to the word paganism, a belief in many gods."

"Bill, since progressive truth gets into totality thinking, these people can be dangerous, can't they? I mean, totality thinking goes in the wrong direction." When Sam realizes what he's saying, he stops short. "You know something, Bill?" he says with a smile. "Something's happened, and I just this minute realized it. Since you alerted me to totality thinking, you've influenced me toward objective truth."

"That's paying attention to influence, Sam."

"I've known all along where you're coming from," says Sam. "You haven't hidden that. But until now, my thinking was 'maybe, maybe not.' Now though, everything comes together, and I know you're right. It's like you say: 'Influences do influence you.'"

"You've heard me repeat that, haven't you?"

"One thing bothers me though, Bill. What if I can't live up to my ideals? Do I have to change worldviews?"

"No, ideals are what you aim toward, Sam."

"Good... I'm so glad I put some things on hold these five years until I could see more clearly. You know if I had a kid brother, I'd tell him to do the same."

"You'll be glad the rest of your life, Sam."

"You said you have another chart. I think you must be holding back something more, something even bigger and better."

"Have I built up enough suspense, Sam?"

"Come on, Bill. Is it about the radical center?"

Chapter 21

YOUR ENTIRE FUTURE AND YOUR PRESENT INTEGRITY
Acting without understanding is like dancing on quicksand

Sam learns more about totality thinking worldviews and their political goals.

While Bill works in his home office at his computer, Sam studies a political chart.

"Bill, how many hours did you spend working on this mother of all charts?"

"Not as many as you'll spend figuring them out."

"What about the circles in the middle?"

"Those are a picture of objective truth with a slash bar through them."

"Slash bar... Oh, that's what that heavy line is. That's like on a 'no smoking' sign. That means the slash says, 'No objective truth allowed here.' So, is that what radical center is all about—fighting against objective truth?"

"You're reading the politics right, Sam."

"Above the slash, the heading says that totality thinking politicizes nonradicals. Hm... That means they get sucked into quicksand because they don't understand." Sam continues to study the chart. *"Bill, I see 'Earth is mother of all' here, but I don't see humanism and New Age. Why are they missing?"*

"Because, this is a political chart," says Bill. *"And strictly speaking, the bottom lines of humanism and New Age are not political. Eventually, however, they can all unite politically because they*

share the single-circle progressive truth view."

"So if the chart is political, Bill, are the circles at the top political groups? Radical cosmology and radical theology sound like religious groups. Isn't theology the study of God?"

"Yes it is" says Bill. "And cosmology is the study of the cosmos, or universe. Sister Miriam represents its radical side. And yes, these groups are political," says Bill. "Politics is what drives them."

"The bottom circles are radical politics for sure."

"Yes," says Bill. "Marxism speaks of the progress of history, fascism talks about the progress of nature or race, and radical center swallows up both of them in its progress of the universe."

"Do we have Marxism and fascism in America?"

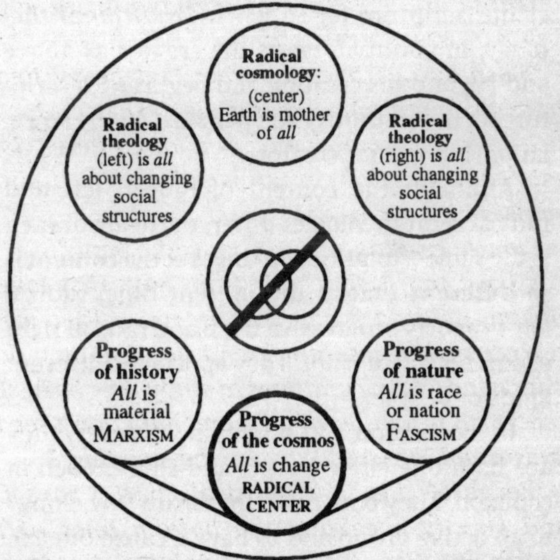

Bill's chart of radical politics without his written explanation

"Not as political parties but as influences."
"Don't radical theologies have names?" Sam asks.
"Yes, but their ideas, their names, and the grouping of their members can change. Also, people in most congregations don't seem to know much about their pastor's theology. And so I like to show basic issues to look for... Here, Sam, read this. This is a simple explanation I wrote about radical theology, left and right."

Radical theology thinks in terms of groups; traditional theology thinks in terms of the individual. *Radical theology, left or right* attacks social problems by reorganizing the political system. It promotes radical political action and claims scripture for support. *Traditional theology,* in contrast, views the creator as above and beyond his creation and begins with scripture as the authority for personal living in relationship to that creator.

Although the content of radical left and radical right theologies differ, the heart of each is the same—totality thinking. Yet the content is so different that at the present time, radical left supports progressive truth and radical right claims objective truth. They appeal to different kinds of people.

In motivation and direction, however, they are both one circle people and share much in common. They both fulfill the desire "to belong" to an active group and to have a cause outside of self. They both romanticize the simple life, especially life before industrial times. More importantly, they both emphasize practice more than belief and process more than content. Finally, both radical theologies depend upon political action to perfect society—for their common final goal is to get rid of human misery by total control of society and of the whole life of individuals. This desired perfect society will be a new order, a utopia, or a so called millenium.

Because they care more about politics than righteous living and care more about action than belief, hardcore right and hardcore left will eventually join with other power holders to meet in a new radical center under a totalitarian system. Carried to its logical conclusion, where else can totality thinking lead?

After Sam finishes reading the explanation, he asks, "Bill, since you talk about theologies, you don't classify as radicals the people of real faith who become active in politics, do you?"

"Absolutely not. There is a difference."

"But what about people who believe very strongly in their cause? Would you say they're radical?"

"No, not at all, Sam. The content of what you believe is what matters, not how strongly you believe it. People with strong convictions should not be labeled radical. You can believe strongly in any position. What you believe is important."

"Then would you say that people of faith are dangerous only to radicals, not to society?"

"That's how I see it, Sam."

"The chart says that radicals unite people by

dealing with crises," says Sam. "Isn't that the same as what I learned at that critical thinking lecture on the Middle East?"

"Yes, Sam, totality thinkers use crises to get more followers. They encourage public fear and chaos because public desperation gives them a chance to present their radical solution. They love crises."

Sam looks at the chart again and reads, "Their new goal becomes to unite a peaceful, protected Earth."

"Yes, that's what everyone wants, of course."

"But what the radicals will give us," says Sam, still looking at the chart, "is a single political party in total power... Bill, I'm puzzled. Why in the world do so many people go along with ideas headed in a radical direction?"

"One reason is people don't understand and don't care about basic core beliefs. We human beings tend to follow personalities and to choose the morality and politics that appeal to our feelings. So we settle into a popular comfort zone with likeminded people and refuse to rouse ourselves to investigate the worldview behind our choices... Besides, Sam, it's not like there are two big, easy-to-see camps out there with a line drawn in the sand between them."

"How is it then?"

"The opposing views we're talking about exist within almost every American group."

"You mean the worldviews don't choose up sides by organizations?"

"That's right. They don't line up in neat packages, Sam. People who live by opposing worldviews work and play side by side."

"What kind of groups are you talking about?"

"You name it. No organization is immune from the drift toward totality thinking, Sam. Differences exist in professional groups and unions, service organizations, clubs, youth organizations..."

"In churches?"

"Yes, Sam, within some places of worship, there are those sympathetic toward each side."

"With a mix from both sides, that makes it difficult to understand what's going on," says Sam.

"No neat packages, Sam."

"Can you clarify all this some way, Bill?"

"Yes, here's something to remember: Think about origins. In spite of all this mixing up on both sides, the origins of the viewpoints are clear and are what count the most. Theism is the origin of objective truth. Remember, you figured this out yourself. You said that if truth never changes, then it would have to begin and end with a being who never changes."

"Hey, I did say that, didn't I?"

"And remember this—rebellion against authority is the root of progressive truth."

"What do you base that on, Bill?"

"On the political radicals' own literature and on my observation. For it's rebelliousness that leads people to choose unworkable, self-destructive paths. You see that in fascist and communist countries and in individual, rebellious lives."

"How do these people square their rebellious acts with their consciences, Bill?"

"Those who encourage violence use as an excuse what they call institutional violence. They say that because existing institutions oppress, then whatever anyone has to do to bring them down is just and right.

And so they attack business, government, ideas..."

"But aren't there also good people involved in that kind of political cause?"

"You know it. Political alignments aren't black and white. They're gray—because human beings are involved."

Sam looks at the chart. "We left out one thing. Outside the circle of acceptance will be all who speak for objective truth."

"So with this blueprint for power in your hands, where will you be, Sam?"

"Outside. An outcast," answers Sam with his head down. Then he looks up quickly, smiles, and adds, "But that won't stop me, Bill."

"Nor will it stop me, Sam. However, if America didn't have good roots—a good beginning and a good history—I'd probably not worry about trying to affect the political outcome."

"But Bill, some people might say it's just a matter of who gets the power, that you could reverse the picture, and single-circle people would be outside."

"History shows that's not true. Under our traditional free enterprise system and constitutional government, we've always been a patchwork of people with room for everyone. And although there have been lapses, this system has benefited everyone the most, better than any other system in history."

"Some people might disagree with you, Bill."

"I'm sure. And, Sam, we can live with disagreement and work out those differences through the right channels and through step by step change."

"What kind of guidelines can you give me?"

"What a question, Sam! Look for unpoliticized

history books, maybe from the early sixties or before that; compare them to new ones. Talk to people. Study hard; read widely; get the dictionary habit. Live by what you know to be right. Then, Sam..."

"Yes?"

"Don't be afraid to express your convictions. If you become informed and if you buck the tide when necessary and try to get along with everyone when it's possible, I can guarantee the best outcome in your life. And you'll be an influence, too."

"Are you a Christian, Bill?"

"Why do you ask?"

"Because if you are, I was wondering how come you haven't ever told me how to become a Christian—especially when I give you so many openings."

"So that's one more thing that has puzzled you, Sam. No, I'm not a Christian, but a lot of my friends are. I'm Jewish. Still, I respect Christians—even their desire for me and others to become Christians because that's part of their faith."

"That's hard for some non-Christians to understand, isn't it, Bill?"

"Yes but not for me. As a Jewish person, I want to stand with those whom society treats unfairly. If they go under, Jewish people will, too."

"Bill, this is the land of the free."

"It's up to you to keep it that way, Sam."

And it's up to you. Your personal future and your country's future depend upon your present integrity—the worldview you follow and the influences you build into your life right now.

Chapter 22

Look Out World Because Here You Come!
If you know where you're going, you can dance free

Sam and Cecelia celebrate their last high school days with Bill by going with him to a movie about Natan Sharansky, a man who challenged the *tyranny* of a totality thinking worldview.

"Nothing they do can humiliate me. I alone can humiliate myself," says Natan Sharansky about the communists as he speaks from the big screen. At this moment the noted Soviet scientist becomes a voice to the outside world for Jewish dissidents—Jewish people who want to leave the Soviet Union. No longer will Sharansky think one thing and say another. No longer can anyone keep him from speaking freely.

The scene shifts to an office where Sharansky in a conversation with a communist official shows how bold he has become. "What I want to say concerns only you," an officer tells Sharansky, "and you must not repeat it to anybody else. If you promise to keep it to yourself, I'll tell you what I know."

"I'm sorry," Sharansky replies, "but I'm much too afraid of your organization to have any secrets with you. Tell me whatever you wish, as long as you understand that as soon as this meeting is over I'll report every word of it."

"Please," the officer pleads, "I really do want to tell you. But you must promise."

"Please," Sharansky answers, "I'd love to know,

believe me. But it will remain a secret only until I reach the first public telephone."

So Sharansky doesn't learn what the great secret is. And he continues to refuse to give specific information about the activities of dissident friends.

Sharansky's boldness finally lands him in prison but fortunately in the first prison he and his fellow prisoner can read great books. In one scene this cellmate advises him, "When Galileo ran into trouble with the authorities, he was smart enough to reverse his stand. He was a great man, not a stubborn one."

"Are you sure he backed down?" Sharansky asks.

"Read it for yourself," the prisoner says as he hands him a book. As Sharansky reads about how pressure brought Galileo to change his stand on a scientific issue, he looks troubled and asks his cellmate to give him time to think about this. He paces the floor while he mumbles to himself, "Am I just being stubborn?"

Finally, the next morning Sharansky faces his fellow prisoner. "I'm ready to debate the issue. What Galileo did was questionable. He may go down in history as a great man, but on this point, he wasn't so great. And I'm not going to make the same mistake. Call me stubborn if you will. I'll debate you, and if Galileo was here, I'd debate him, too. I won't let him break my spirit. Besides I have more to stand on than a scientific theory. I'm standing for what I know to be morally right."

At the end of the movie, Sharansky, after years in prison, reunites with his wife, Avital, in Israel. On a starlit night on a flat-roof building in an Israeli city, he talks to her about his greatest struggle. "In prison," he tells her, "I was able to take a strong stand when my own welfare was at stake, but when the Soviets threatened to harm you because of my resistance, I wondered if I was doing the right thing. How could I make you suffer?"

"What did you finally decide?" Avital asks him.

"It wasn't easy, but I finally came to the conclusion that our lives are intertwined and that I had to make my difficult decisions about your suffering the same as for myself."

With that news, Avital hugs Natan and expresses her understanding. "I'm so glad. That was my prayer for you. If you had betrayed yourself for my sake, you would have betrayed me as well."

When Sam puts his hand on Cecelia's arm, she smiles as they share the dramatic moment.

Then Avital asks a question: "Was there any happy time for you in prison, Natan?"

"Yes, I learned you can be free even there. I remember one time in particular because it was the happiest time in my life until now. I was in a punishment cell for refusing to cooperate in the labor camp, and my cellmate was a Christian. He had his Bible and I had the book of Psalms that you gave me. We had them just because we had each in our own circumstances raised such a ruckus about keeping them. That month of reading and talking together in those worst of circumstances was my happiest time of all. Would you believe that?"

"I believe it because I understand," Avital says.

"And Avital—about my happiness in prison—my bond with you was stronger than my isolation and my inner freedom more powerful than my external bondage." He takes Avital in his arms and kisses her. Then after they stand together looking over the quiet city, Natan says, "You don't know how many times I dreamed of this moment."

Walking out of the theater, Bill, Sam, and Cecelia are quiet as they hold to themselves the drama and tenderness of those last moments.

Finally, approaching their car, Sam breaks the silence. "You know, don't you, that Mom wants all of us to go to our house afterwards?"

"I'm glad," Cecelia says, "because I'd like to hear more about what you guys think about the movie."

Settled down in Sam's living room after a snack, the three of them talk about scenes from the movie.

"I liked it when Sharansky stood up to that prison officer and said he wouldn't keep any secrets the prison keeper would tell him," says Sam.

"Why do you think he did that, Sam?" Bill asks.

"He wasn't going to give anyone power over himself. He was drawing a line in the sand, making it clear where he stood."

"And he went further than that, too, Sam," says Bill. "Later he refused to give out information that might hurt the Jewish cause. He gave out only general information that was not secret anyway."

"Doesn't that apply to what you've talked about, Bill?" Cecelia asks.

"Yes. Has Sam talked to you about the power someone gains over you by getting personal information about you?"

"Yes, he explained about being a gatekeeper of information," she says. "I decided it's important to be open with public people and not afraid to give out general information but to think twice about giving out personal information."

"So you understand... You know, what I liked tonight was how Sharansky stood up to Galileo."

"That's not as gutsy as how he stood up to real live people, is it?" Sam asks. "In those cases he knew he was going to suffer for what he did."

"I think he deserves even more credit in this case," Bill answers. "There are a couple of reasons I say that. First of all, he had to reexamine his position. And believe me, at times you have to reconsider your position to make sure you're on the right track. But like with Sharansky, every time you get through a crisis, you come out stronger and with clearer vision. And my second reason is that with Galileo, it was harder for Sharansky to recognize the issue, which was: Am I going to continue to stand for what I believe, or should I stop resisting? If Sharansky had not seen the issue clearly, he could have lost heart by what he heard about Galileo's adjustment to his circumstances, so to speak.

"Let me give you an example from Sharansky's own book to show you how important it is to recognize something that will steer you off course. One time Sharansky overheard officer Chernysh talking to his wife about an evening at the Bolshoi Theatre. And another time he heard him ask his son, 'Did you finish your homework?' Seeing the human side of this official made Sharansky think that maybe he had been too hard on the leaders—for after all they are human beings."

"How could there be anything wrong with seeing the human side of these people?" Cecelia asks.

"It's always good to realize that all other people are human like ourselves, but in this case Sharansky recognized the real issue he faced, which was this: Would he resist the evil of the totalitarian system with all his strength, or would he let his will be weakened?"

"Just from what he overheard, I never would have thought to look for a bigger issue," says Sam.

"You have to learn to pay attention, Sam, because influence works its greatest harm when you don't know you're being influenced. Look at all the good people who go to Congress and end up playing the political game like everyone else. They start out with good intentions but fall into the same shady practices of their famous and prestigious friends there. And you face the same kind of problem. In classroom groups or outside of school, when you see the human side—or even the admirable side—of people who do things that you know are wrong, your convictions weaken, guaranteed... that is, unless you actively resist their influence. And if you have a choice about whom you listen to, then it's not a matter of resisting influence but of choosing whose influence you place yourself under. For if you don't even recognize influences and issues, you'll allow your ideals to rust away for sure."

"Yeah," Sam says. "In the movie, the prisoner who betrayed himself and others didn't even survive."

"Without moral principles," says Bill, "how could he buck the tide? Now let me tell you about what happened in the book after the movie ended."

"Good. There's more," says Cecelia.

"In prison, Sharansky could see the big picture

because prison forced him to face issues and to find meaning in life. But after he lived in freedom in Israel, he says he got lost in all the choices of ordinary living. Life became complicated and he found he had no time to reflect on the bigger questions... So if a mature man like Sharansky has trouble sorting out life after all he's been through, it's no wonder you guys struggle to find your way."

"But, Bill, thanks to you, Cecelia and I and some of our friends have begun to take time to think about bigger questions. And that movie tonight was the perfect ending for our times with you. It's easier to understand what we've been talking about when we see it lived out in someone else's life."

"Bill, you've been a big help to us, and the movie was inspiring," Cecelia adds.

"Romantic too, huh?" Sam asks as he moves closer to her on the sofa.

"Let me jump in here with what I want to say, Bill," Mrs. Ming says as she dries her hands from cleaning up the kitchen after the late snack.

"We hardly knew each other when I asked you to come over and talk to Sam about that upsetting film that day. I can't tell you how much I appreciate your influence on him and his friends since that time."

This is your babushka signing off. You're on your own now, so let me leave you with this final thought: Don't keep looking over your shoulder at those who oppose you, and don't look for an easy path. Instead focus straight ahead and keep going. *For if you know where you're going, you can dance free.*

Look out world because here you come!

NOTES

You will notice that although characters and their reactions are
fictitious, many of the happenings were real events.
Reference numbers were left out of text to avoid distraction.

Chapter 1: Where are you headed?
9-11   Journal entry. Fictitious but based on current feeling-
centered group activities
13   ...FREEDOM WOULD HAVE BEEN IMPOSSIBLE HAD NOT
THE BABUSHKAS WORKED BEHIND THE SCENES...
"[Babushkas] represent the only remaining moral authority
in post-Soviet society... 'We babushkas have been alive
practically since the revolution. We know the difference
between right and wrong,' said a seventy-one year old
Russian woman" (Carroll 1992)."

Chapter 2: The power of suggestion
14   THE ONLY TIME I FEEL CHINESE.   Taken from a similar
remark by an American with an Asian heritage.
15-17   Lecture by Steven Smith, a fictitious character, is taken
from notes on lecture and demonstration given by Father
Kent Burtner in Orange, California (Burtner 1991).
18   The section on using seeing and hearing words reflects
how someone gains trust (Bandler 1991).
19   *STAGES* (Activity sheet 235). These activity sheets are not
in *Books in Print* but were in public school use recently.
Activities are based on stages of dying outlined by Elisab-
eth Kubler Ross. MARIE BEGINS TO TALK IN A SLOW,
DREAMY VOICE WITH HER EYES CLOSED. Marie closed her
eyes, but facilitators in these activities do not close their eyes.
They watch the reactions of participants.

Chapter 3: Activities and awareness
22   MEDITATION, RELAXATION TECHNIQUES,
VISUALIZING, MAGIC THINKING, ROLE PLAYING,
GUIDED IMAGERY. Suhor, a leading educator writing in
Education Week, a major education publication,
encourages "the use of silence" in the classroom. For
teaching various subjects, he recommends guided imagery,

visualizing, meditation, stopping inner thoughts, witnessing one's consciousness, and observing one's breathing through relaxation and stress management exercises (Suhor 1992).

23 Excerpt is a summary of a passage in *Snapping*. (Conway and Siegelman 1979, 1978).

25 ...YOU MAY EVEN BE INFLUENCED TOWARD MURDER AND SUICIDE... (Dare, William 1985).

25 RECORDS SHOW THAT ROLE PLAYING SOMETIMES TRIGGERS EMOTIONAL REACTIONS ... "We spoke with a number of individuals who reported experiencing overwhelming discomfort, anxiety, and even intense snapping moments during role playing and psychodrama" (Conway and Siegelman 1979, 1978, 168).

26 PRECAUTION: *NEVER USE ANY OF THESE EXERCISES...* This section is a quotation from Marilee Zdenek's book on guided imagery (1987).

26 Guided imagery activity described (Zdenek 1987).

26 YOU LET SOMETHING WONDERFUL APPEAR BEFORE YOU... This section is a quotation (Zdenek 1987).

Chapter 4: Group power

29 The story about Denise is based on testimony by Jacqueline Lawrence in a hearing before the State Department of Education in Washington, D.C. (Schlafly 1984, 426-428). Although this incident happened in Maryland, the author heard of a similar local incident. Lawrence says purpose of exercise seems to be to gain greater group unity.

30 Story about Harry (Redl et al. 1991).

32 ...THOSE WHO GET ATTENTION ARE THE REBELS, RISK-TAKERS, AND JOKERS... (Witty 1983).

32, 33 Summary of *AMONG THE THUGS* (Buford 1992).

33 A REVIEWER OF THE BOOK SAID... (Jones 1992).

33, 34 Summary of *ORDINARY MEN* (Browning 1992).

35 MEMBERSHIP IN A GROUP CAN BECOME MORE IMPORTANT TO YOU THAN LIFELONG BELIEFS (Leerhsen 1991).

35 AUTHOR-ENGLISHMAN W. ROSS ASHBY SAYS THAT THE BRAIN ARRANGES ITSELF ACCORDING TO EXPERIENCE (Conway and Siegelman 1979, 1978, 131)

Chapter 5: Death and sex

37 THEN IF DESENSITIZING TEARS DOWN THOSE

BARRIERS, THERE'S TROUBLE. "There were good reasons for mankind to place sexual inhibitions on itself. It was the price we had to pay for the development of family, society, and culture" (Bettelheim 1979, 370).

37 DESENSITIZE. Emphasizes importance (Kilpatrick 1985).

37 ...MARK TWAIN. HE TALKED ABOUT HOW HE WAS DESENSITIZED (Kantrow 1987).

38 WITH AN INFECTED PERSON, THE ODDS ARE TOO HIGH, SAM—EVEN WITH A CONDOM EVERY TIME. Sex with infected persons, even with 100 percent condom use, causes one in three to contract AIDS, writes Dr. Margaret A. Fischl in JAMA, the Journal of the American Medical Association, February 1987 (Los Angeles Times August 1987) as reported in Safe Sex brochure of Grapevine Publications in Boise, Idaho.

38 ARE YOU SURE YOU WANT TO TRUST YOUR LIFE TO A BALLOON? (Womanity 1987)

39 REPARATIVE THERAPY IS ONE METHOD THAT SUPPORTS YOUR DESIRE TO CHANGE [HOMOSEXUAL BEHAVIOR] (Nicolosi 1991).

40 OF THOSE WHO TRY SUICIDE, MOST ARE JUST DEPRESSED... NINETY PERCENT NEVER TRY AGAIN... (Allen 1986 and several other authorities).

41 ...ABOUT FIFTEEN YEAR OLD GIRLS. NOW - 26 PERCENT ENGAGE IN PREMARITAL SEX... (Recent news sources).

Chapter 6: Family ties

43 LEARNING TO REFOCUS YOU-MESSAGES INTO I-MESSAGES... (Gordon 1974).

44 DEAR DAD, I WANT YOU TO KNOW... Paraphrased, condensed letter (Smalley 1988).

44 A CHILD OF DIVORCE IS MORE LIKELY TO HAVE EMOTIONAL PROBLEMS OR LEARNING DISABILITIES; MORE LIKELY TO COMMIT SUICIDE OR CRIME (Klein 1992).

45 AND ACCORDING TO PSYCHOLOGIST JAY HALEY, THIS INTERFERENCE CAN UPSET FAMILY AUTHORITY AND CREATE UNHEALTHY CONFLICT (Haley 1976)

Chapter 7: Your future family and your present life

47 SAM AND CECELIA LISTEN TO A SCHOOL ASSEMBLY SPEAKER. Tim Stafford speaks in school assemblies across the country. The comments here, however, are from

his book (Stafford 1988).

50 TO PREVENT PROBLEMS LISTEN TO KATHLEEN
    HONEYCUTT, GUEST FAMILY LIFE LECTURER
    (Honeycutt 1991).

51 THAT WAS TRUE FOR LYNDA BARRY... (Barry 1991).

Chapter 8: Your culture

53 Environmental film in this story is an actual film used to
    change attitudes (Eakman 1991). See note for page 70.

Chapter 9: Cults, totality thinking, and information

59-65 Understanding of cults gained by author over the years.
       Some information is from Steven Hassan's *Cult Mind
       Control* (1988).

59 Destructive cult definition (Hassan 1988).

59 Waco incident in news in spring 1993

60 INFORMATION DISEASE (Conway and Siegelman 1979,
    1978, 136).

64 Information on the page down to the last paragraph, which
    begins WHY ARE DESTRUCTIVE CULTS ALLOWED TO
    EXIST? (Conway and Siegelman 1979, 1978).

Chapter 10: You, the gatekeeper of information

66 Page about Nazi moral dilemma (Peikoff 1982).

67, 68 SPACESHIP GAME. An actual choice made by a friend and
        the actual reaction at a state university. This survival
        activity comes in many forms such as lifeboat game or
        fallout shelter game. In any case, players have to choose
        who will live to repopulate the planet—and who will die.

67 HANNAH ARENDT, AN AUTHORITY ON TOTALITARIAN-
    ISM... (Peikoff 1982).

68 Page about moral dilemmas. Christina Sommers (1991),
    ethics professor, says moral dilemmas should not be the
    starting point nor the end when talking about moral
    standards. Straight talk about morals, she says, is not
    brainwashing because brainwashing makes you less able
    to reason and have good judgment whereas moral teaching
    improves your ability to reason and to be responsible.

70 Anita Hoge and attitudinal remediation. Anita Hoge's son
    Garrett was upset by the same environmental film that
    Sam experienced in chapter eight. After the film, Garret's
    group played a survival game (Eakman 1991).

70 A paraphrased list of what attitudinal testing looks for

(Eakman 1991).

71 School-based clinics and peer counseling (Cleary 1975).
John Cleary (1975) found that the early program of peer
counseling held training meetings at Planned Parenthood
of New York. For more information about school-based
clinics, see Richard Glasow's book (1988).

Chapter 11: Freedom and totalitarianism

72-74 This story is based on knowledge gained from teaching a
year in mainland China. See bibliography for author's
book, *CHINA: The Lion and the Dragon.*

76 THEN, AFTER THE RULING POLITICAL PARTY
REPLACES THE MORAL AUTHORITY OF THE FAMILY
AND ORGANIZED RELIGION, IT SETS UP A NEW SOCIAL
MORALITY... MORALITY BECOMES POLITICAL
INSTEAD OF PERSONAL. "In the United States, we
ordinarily think of this [child-rearing] responsibility as
centered in the family, with the parents playing the
decisive part... Not so in the Union of Soviet Socialist
Republics" (Bronfenbrenner 1970).

Chapter 12: A new authority

77-78 Schoolboard event. Mrs. Ming and Sam are fictitious
characters, but the event was real.

79 Insufficient food supply was predicted by Paul Ehrlich
(1968) in his book, *The Population Bomb.*

79,80 Julian Simond's research (Simond 1991).

80 INFORMATION MAKES POSSIBLE... (McLuhan 1964)

Chapter 13: Future freedom and present thinking

82-84 skills   Mr. Burt is the story name for the real Professor
Richard Paul. The lecture and audience participation are
an accurate re-creation of the event (Paul 1990).

85 List at bottom of page is from an activist manual. First line
says, LEARN TO SEPARATE IDEAS FROM FEELINGS...
(Michels et al. 1991). The organization that puts out the
manual is associated with Frances Moore Lappé (1991).

Chapter 14: Living with change

92 AYN RAND. Reference to another book: (Rand 1974).

Chapter 15: Integrating ideas

94 ...THE SCHOOLBOARD TOLD MR. WASHINGTON HE

COULDN'T TAKE HIS BIBLE WITH HIM... This is based on
a similar incident.

98 THE HUMANITAS PROGRAM. Quotations accurate
although reference source unavailable at present.

99 OR LATER WHEN YOU GO...and rest of paragraph about
integrated university courses. (Moyers 1989).

Chapter 16: Resisting harm

102 "YOU CAN FEEL IT COMING ON," HE SAYS. "YOU START
DOUBTING YOURSELF... Deprogrammer Ted Patrick had
this experience (Conway and Siegelman 1979, 1978).

Chapter 17: Your total environment

104-108 YOUR TOTAL ENVIRONMENT (MacGillis 1988 tapes)

Chapter 18: A new prejudice

111, 112 Paraphrased and condensed from lecture in California at
Santa Rosa Junior College (Foster 1989).

Chapter 19: Worldviews in conflict

NO REFERENCES

Chapter 20: Looking for core beliefs

123 NOW AS TO HOW I COME TO MY CONCLUSIONS?
USUALLY I START WITH A QUESTION IN MY MIND.
Sternberg in *Psychology Today* describes the mind of the
puzzler (Sternberg 1982) and the mind of the author in
solving puzzles about the trends of the times.

124 ... ACCORDING TO A FRIEND WHO OWNS A
BOOKSTORE, WE'RE NOW IN A NEW PHASE. NEW AGE
BOOKS WON'T BE SHELVED AS NEW AGE OR OCCULT...
Article from *Publishers Weekly* (Elie 1992).

124 ...EASTERN RELIGION IS GIVING WAY TO FOLK
RELIGION... BOOKS ABOUT RELIGIONS OF OTHER
CULTURES ARE POPULAR IN THE CLASSROOM... This
was my observation at the 1992 American School
Librarians Association convention in Baltimore.

Chapter 21: Your entire future and your present integrity   NO REFERENCES

Chapter 22: Look out world because here you come!

134-140 Fictitious movie is based on real book (Sharansky 1988).

SELECTED BIBLIOGRAPHY

Allen, Robert Raymond. 1986. The Suicide Lobby.
Washington, D.C.: Teen Suicide Prevention Taskforce.

Bandler, Richard and John Grinder. 1979. *Frogs into
Princes*. Moab, UT: Real People Press.

Barry, Lynda. 1991. Guardian neighbor (Special Summer).
Newsweek

Bettelheim, Bruno. 1979, 1952. *Surviving and Other Essays*.
New York, NY: Vintage Books, Random House.

Bronfenbrenner, Urie. 1970. *Two Worlds of Childhood: U.S.
and U.S.S.R.* New York, NY: Touchstone Book.

Browning, Christopher. 1992. *Ordinary Men*. New York,
NY: Aaron Asher Books, Harper Collins.

Buford, Bill. 1992. *Among the Thugs*. New York, NY:
Norton.

Burtner, Kent. 1991. Lecture. Orange, CA: St.
Joseph Presents Radio conference.

Cleary, John. 1975. *Classroom Sex Education*. No publisher
listing.

Conway, Flo and Jim Siegelman. 1979, 1978. *Snapping:
America's epidemic of sudden personality change*. New
York, NY: Delta of Dell Publishing.

Dear, William. 1985. *The Dungeon Master*. New York, NY:
Ballantine of Random House.

Eakman, B. K. 1991. *Educating for the New World Order*.
Portland, OR: Halcyon Press.

Elie, Paul. 1992. Horizon 2000 (December 7). *Publishers
Weekly*.

Ehrlich, Paul, 1968. *The Population Bomb*. New York, NY:
Ballantine Books.

Evans, Pearl. 1988. *CHINA: The Lion and the Dragon*.
Petaluma, CA: Small Helm Press.

Fischl, Margaret. 1987. Sex with infected persons, even
with 100% condom use, causes one in three to contract
AIDS. February 1987. *Journal of the American Medical
Association* reported in August 1987 Los Angeles

Times and recorded in Safe Sex brochure. Boise, ID: *Grapevine Publications.*

Foster, Leota. 1989. Lecture: The theology of wife-battering. Santa Rosa, CA: Santa Rosa Junior College.

Glasow, Richard. 1988. *School-Based Clinics, the Abortion Connection.* Washington, D.C.: National Right to Life Educational Trust Fund.

Gordon, Thomas. 1974. *Teacher Effectiveness Training (T.E.T.).* New York, NY: Peter H. Wyden Publisher.

Haley, Jay. 1976. *Problem Solving Therapy.* New York, NY: Harper Colophon Books, Harper & Row.

Hassan, Steven. 1988. *Combatting Cult Mind Control.* Rochester, VT: Park Street Press.

Honeycutt, Kathleen. 1991. Lecture: What were you doing the first nine months of your life (August 16)? Sunnyvale, CA: California Prolife Council State Convention.

Jones, Malcolm, Jr. 1992. Far into the madding crowd (June 1). *Newsweek.*

Kantrow, Alan M. 1987. *The Constraints of Corporate Tradition.* New York, NY: Perennial Library, Harper & Row.

Kilpatrick, William Kirk. 1985. *The Emperor's New Clothes: the naked truth about the new psychology.* Westchester, IL: Crossway Books.

Klein, Joe. 1992. *Whose Values* (June 8). *Newsweek.*

Lappé, Frances Moore.1989. *Rediscovering America's Values.* New York, NY: Ballantine Books.

——1991. Break the habit of issuing manifestos. *The Progressive.*

Leerhsen, Charles. Special Summer 1991. Helping themselves. *Newsweek.*

MacGillis, Miriam. 1988. Tapes from teachers' workshop in Santa Rosa, CA: *Education for a small planet.* Sonoma, CA: Global Perspectives.

McLuhan, Marshall. 1964.*Understanding Media: The extensions of man.* New York, NY: Signet Books.

Michels, Peg and Suzanne Paul. 1991. *Making the Rules.* Minneapolis, MN: Project Public Life.

Nicolosi, Joseph. 1991. *Reparative Therapy of Male Homosexuality*. Northvale, NJ: Jason Aronson, Inc.

Paul, Richard. 1990. *Critical Thinking*. Sonoma State University, Rohnert Park, CA: Center for Critical Thinking and Moral Critique.

———1990. Lecture: Critical thinking about the Middle East (December 11). Petaluma, CA.

Peikoff, Leonard. 1982. *The Ominous Parallels: The End of Freedom in America*. New York, NY: New American Library.

Schlafly, Phyllis, ed. 1984. *Child Abuse in the Classroom. Official Transcript of Proceedings before U.S. Office of Education in Washington, D.C.* Alton, IL: Pere Marquette Press.

Sears, Alan. 1991. Lecture. Luther Burbank Center, Santa Rosa CA: Citizens Leading Effective Action Now.

Sharansky, Natan. 1988. *Fear No Evil*. New York, NY: Random House.

Simond, Julian. 1991. Lecture KQED August 26: Population, resources, and the environment: good trends and bad thinking (August 2). San Francisco, CA: The Commonwealth Club.

Smalley, Gary. 1988. *The Language of Love*. Pomona, CA: Focus on the Family.

Sommers, Christina Hoff. 1991. Teaching the virtues (November). Hillsdale, MI: *Imprimis*.

Stafford, Tim. 1988. *Worth the Wait*. Wheaton, IL: Tyndale House.

Sternberg, Robert and Janet Davidson. 1982. The mind of the puzzler (June). *Psychology Today*.

Suhor, Charles. 1992. The uses of silence (January 29). *Education Week*.

Witty, Susan. 1983. The laugh-makers (August). *Psychology Today*.

Womanity brochure. 1987. First aid for AIDS. Pleasant Hill, CA: Womanity.

Zdenek, Marilee. 1987. *Inventing the Future: Advances in Imagery that Can Change Your Life*. New York, NY: McGraw-Hill Book Co.

GLOSSARY

abstinence—refraining from; often used in regard to sex

agenda— a plan; sometimes used to mean a hidden plan

all is one and one is all—a New Age belief that everything in the universe is connected and equal in worth

altered state of consciousness—concentrated attention turned inward; ranges from daydreaming to a trance state

attitudinal testing—testing to determine emotional reactions, value system, and center of control of person tested

authoritarian—unlike authority, has a negative connotation—implies abuse of authority

authority—the life center to which an individual looks for guidance and meaning

authority figures—examples: parents, teachers, policemen

babushka—Russian grandmother

bigoted—stubborn; intolerant; narrow minded; often used to describe those with whom someone disagrees

capitalism—a free enterprise economy; also called a free market system; based on voluntary participation

censorship—government restriction of speech or dissent

coalition—used here to mean the act of siding with a person or group against another person or group

comprehensive education—education that teaches the whole person through the total environment

conflict resolution—a method to resolve conflict; the use of you-messages as opposed to I-messages to express non-threatening personal feelings

content—in education, subject matter; *see* process. In other areas, substance, as in "style over substance"

cosmology—study of the universe

cosmos—a harmonious universe

counter-culture—a culture that bucks the value system of the establishment or tradition.

cult, destructive—a group that demands total control of individuals in the group

cult exit counselor—one who counsels ex-cult members,

usually on a voluntary basis

damage control—as used here, the handling of uninvited, unwanted influences

deprogrammer—one who helps rehabilitate ex-cult members by looking for the lie believed and forcing the person to think

desensitize—make emotionally insensitive; change usual reactions

disintegrate—collapse, deteriorate; used in this text about the disorganization of personality.

dissenters—those who express disagreement with leadership or public opinion

ecology—the totality of relations between organisms and their environment. Also used in this writing to speak of the ecology within a human culture

ethnic —a member of a minority group who keep their cultural background

ethnocentrism—an attitude by a person that sees his or her own cultural group as superior

euphemisms—words or phrases coined to make an unacceptable idea seem acceptable

euthanasia—mercy killing

facilitator—one who leads a group in a nondirective way

fantasy—in imagination

fascism—a system that when put into practice has proven to be totalitarian

Gaia—a popular earth goddess of Greek myths

gatekeeping—as used here, being aware of and in control of incoming influences and outgoing personal information

group consensus—agreement within a group attained by persuasion or by yielding of individuals to the group will

guided imagery—a fantasy experience in an altered state of consciousness, which is led by someone other than participant; sometimes involves a spirit guide

Holocaust—the systematic slaughter of six million Jewish people in Nazi Germany

humanism—a wide range of beliefs that place human relationships as most important

hypnosis—a practice that brings change in the quality and focus of a person's attention and which changes his or

her inner and outer experience. The hypnotized person
   becomes more open to suggestions from the hypnotist
ideological—relating to a system of concepts, especially
   about human life or culture
information disease—the failure of the brain and nervous
   system to process information properly
institutional violence—a claim made by political radicals
   that institutions and existing authority are violent because they oppress; an excuse by radicals for violence
integrated learning—the combination of subject matter under a unifying theme or belief, or under a worldview.
interpretation—an explanation from one point of view
intrusion by government—interference by government in
   private living
inventories—direct questions to be answered about your
   feelings, attitudes, interests, abilities
manipulate—to use power to make others act in ways that a
   group or individual desires
Marxism—a system that when put into practice has proven
   to be totalitarian
meditation—in traditional meaning, active thinking about
   spiritual truth; in current popular use, emptying the mind
   and entering an altered state of consciousness
monitor reactions—to be aware of and observe self
   reactions
moral dilemma—a situation that seems to have no good moral solution
New Age—a wide range of beliefs borrowed from many
   sources; formerly called occult.
objective truth—an unchangeable standard that exists apart
   from ideas in your own mind
occult—literally means hidden, but commonly used to speak
   of contact with the spirit world
oppress—treat unjustly under a heavy hand of power
paganism—ancient belief in polytheism, or many gods
patriarchal—man-centered.; now usually used negatively
personality—used here to mean the will, mind, and emotions of an individual
philosophy—in its broad sense, a worldview; a view of life

that explains life's fundamental questions

political activism—taking part in political activities, such as giving out pamphlets, calling political leaders, demonstrating, etc.

political correctness—a standard for conduct and beliefs; used to change the public at large through language, labels, and rules; redefines old terms

politicizing—forcing people into political reaction, sometimes by lure or intimidation. Forcing political debate on issues

premarital sex—sex before marriage

premise—a belief, either proved or unproved, upon which something is based

principle—a truth that is foundational and that can be applied to different situations

process—a method, procedure, or way of life. Process emphasized over content means how something is done is more important than what is done

progressive truth—changing truth based upon changing social consensus

radical—extremist

radical center—political unifying of radical right and radical left through earth-centered cosmology; control of population a major theme

radical theology—focuses on changing social structures, or the way society organizes itself; more interested in politics and sociology than anything else

role playing—play acting to learn ways to react to given situations

secondary virginity—abstaining from sex until marriage by starting from the present moment regardless of the past

social consensus—group agreement

social morality—a changing standard of morality based upon group standards; the group is more important than the individual

social structures—the organization and relationships of groups in a society

solidarity—comradely support

spirit guide—an imaginary guide during a visualization or

guided imagery; a guide from the spirit world
spiritual—having to do with the spirit
state, the—often used to mean the national government
suggestible—open to suggestions without resistance
survival game—an activity that begins with the premise that
    overpopulation calls for elimination of some people on
    the planet; participants must decide who will live to re-
    populate the planet—and who will die
theism—belief in a creator God who is separate and apart
    from creation but in control of it and above and beyond it.
theology—the study of God
totalitarianism—the political concept that the citizen should
    be totally subject to an absolute state authority
totality thinking—a belief by a group that its members know
    what is good for all others; a belief that the world can be
    made better by social control; a belief that tends toward
    elimination of private life
tradition—continuity of a culture through patterns of
    thought or action
traditional theology—belief in theism. *See* theism
tyranny—heavy-handed, unjust power
visualization—an activity in imagination that sometimes
    creates an altered, or dream, state
vulnerability—a state of being open to harm
worldview—a view of the world from a particular starting
    point; a philosophy

INDEX

ABOUT THE AUTHOR

For seventeen years, educator Pearl Evans enjoyed teaching—ten years in public schools and seven years to adults. Adult teaching included English in China a year, English to Indochinese-Americans a year, and adult Bible literature in a public school district five years.

Since returning from China, author Evans now enjoys writing. And babushka Evans likes to hear from her readers. You can write her at Small Helm Press, 622-A Baker Street, Petaluma, California 94952.